RESCUE

OUR BEST AMERICA IS ONLY
ONE GENERATION AWAY

AMERICA

RESCUE

OUR BEST AMERICA IS ONLY
ONE GENERATION AWAY

AMERICA

CHRIS SALAMONE
AND PROFESSOR GILBERT MORRIS

GREENLEAF
BOOK GROUP PRESS

Published by Greenleaf Book Group Press
Austin, Texas
www.gbgpress.com

Distributed by Greenleaf Book Group LLC

For ordering information or special discounts for bulk purchases, please contact Greenleaf Book Group LLC at PO Box 91869, Austin, TX 78709, 512.891.6100.

Design and composition by Greenleaf Book Group LLC
Cover design by Greenleaf Book Group LLC

Publisher's Cataloging-In-Publication Data
(Prepared by The Donohue Group, Inc.)
Salamone, Chris M.
    Rescue America : our best America is only one generation away / Chris M. Salamone and Gilbert Morris. — 1st ed.
    p. : ill., charts ; cm.
    ISBN: 978-1-60832-141-4

    1. Political culture—United States. 2. Social values—United States. 3. Youth—Political activity—United States. 4. United States—Politics and government—21st century. 5. United States—Social conditions—21st century. I. Morris, Gilbert, 1965- II. Title.
JA75.7 .S25 2011
306.2   2011933294

Part of the Tree Neutral® program, which offsets the number of trees consumed in the production and printing of this book by taking proactive steps, such as planting trees in direct proportion to the number of trees used: www.treeneutral.com

TreeNeutral®

Printed in the United States of America on acid-free paper

11 12 13 14 15 10 9 8 7 6 5 4 3 2 1

First Edition

CONTENTS

ACKNOWLEDGMENTS

Special thanks and recognition to those who have been such incredibly supportive and influential figures in my life:

- My father, Anthony: For your never-ending support, inspiration, and unconditional love—you are the wind beneath my wings. Words cannot possibly express the love and gratitude that I feel for all you have given to me, unselfishly, every single day of my life.

- My mother, Rita, God rest your soul: For giving me fifteen years of love and teaching me the values of respect, kindness, and integrity.

- My sister, Karen: For your constant love and support, and for pouring your heart and soul into helping build my businesses. I'm blessed to have you as a sister. I love you very much. Beauty and brains—who says you can't have it all?!

- My great-grandparents, Antonino and Lucia (who, out of respect, was always referred to as "Donna Lucia"): For making the long journey to America in 1903 with only twenty dollars in their pockets and the shirts on their backs. Without your courage and sacrifice, our family history would be very different.

- My grandparents, Leondina and Cristenzio Salamone, and my Aunt Rose (every Italian family has an Aunt Rose, but mine was very special): For living the American dream every day, and making our past, present, and future possible. Salute a la famiglia!

- Gilbert Morris, one of my closest friends and a colleague for the past seventeen years: For your friendship and unmatched knowledge of history and philosophy. This book would not have been possible without your support and collaboration. While we do not always agree, you are one of the world's truly great thinkers and will always be my brother.

- Mark Gensheimer: For your steadfast friendship in good times and tough times. I am truly blessed to call you my dear friend and to be godfather to your children.

- Lt. Col. Dan Colfax, Sgt. Peter Gary, and Lt. Col. Stuart Jolly: With gratitude not only for your friendship and unquestioned support over the years, but also for your committed service to this great nation. It is an honor to count you among my closest of friends.

- Kim Marjenhoff, Alice Branton, and Carolyn Sampson: For being such an important part of my life—friendships that last a lifetime are an amazing blessing.

- Scot Brands: For your dedication, honesty, character, and most of all your friendship.

- Doc and Mrs. Colfax: For your constant encouragement. I'm where I am because you believed in me and, on a single word, enrolled me in an LSAT course. The rest is now history.

- Cara C.: For your unconditional friendship and love, even when I didn't deserve it.

- Trudi Rossi: Thank you, maestro, for your coaching, confidence, and patience; and for inspiring me further in my passion for singing opera.

- Donna P.: For always believing in me and seeing the best in me.

- Steven Sinopoli: For your support and guidance over the years.

- Kathryn J.: For your patience and unselfish support during the long and arduous months of the early writings of this book.

- Doug Miller: All my thoughts and prayers are with you. Once day at a time, my friend.

- Kevin S.: For your guidance and wisdom in the world of publishing and speaking. And Keri, who makes all the trains run on time.

- Brent C. and Kevin S.: For your amazing dedication and creativity—you guys are the best of the best!

- St. Anselm College: For providing me with an outstanding education and a foundation based in faith. And to the St. A's basketball program (particularly Coach Ted Paulauskas and Coach "Ducky" Mead for your guidance and principled leadership).

- To the thousands of staff members and the tens of thousands of students that I have had the privilege of working with over the years at LeadAmerica, the National Student Leadership Conference, and the BarBri-NILE Law School Prep Program: Thank you for your enthusiasm and for always being an inspiration for me to keep working to make a difference in the world. You are all truly significant!

- To our heavenly Father and Creator: All honor and glory are yours!

PART I

Then:
The Dawn *of a* Dynasty

THE DAWN OF A DYNASTY

"Consider your origin: you were not born to live like brutes, but to follow virtue and knowledge," wrote the eminent Italian poet Dante Alighieri. It was counsel given during a time, the late Middle Ages, when one's origin was not an uncommon consideration. Much of Europe, including Dante's Italy, was in political and spiritual crisis following the Crusades and had yet to find its footing during the Renaissance, for which his hometown of Florence would become best known. Dante's counsel from his famous *Divine Comedy* was certainly timely, even prophetic, given the state of his country at that time. His homeland needed to—and would, shortly after his death in 1321— return to its spiritual, classical roots.

Dante's words were also timeless. They point to a transcendent truth: that all collective progress is merely an outcrop of individual progress. For any group of people—especially one as large as a country—to recover from any crisis, its citizens need to return to the foundational virtues and knowledge that establish all enduring human institutions.

It is now no coincidence that the national heritage of the man known as the "father of the Italian language" and "the Supreme Poet" includes preeminence in two global institutions: family and the arts. While Italians are known for many interests, foremost among them are a deep love and respect of family and a deep appreciation of the arts. As the great-grandson of Italian immigrants, I am a beneficiary of both. And, as an American citizen, I am also blessed to be the beneficiary of another heritage—one that was established less than three hundred years ago yet has bettered more lives and improved more economies than any national heritage in history.

It is therefore of great interest to me—an Italian-American heir—that my American heritage is facing a spiritual, political crisis not dissimilar to that in Dante's fourteenth-century Italy. The advice he gave then is thus fitting for America, and Americans, today.

We must consider our origin so that we can once again follow our foundational virtue and knowledge. It is the way America became a great nation and the way Americans were meant to live.

My great grandparents, Antonio and Lucia Salamone, in New Jersey in the early 1950's
with family members including my father (second from left).

This ship's manifest lists my great grandparents and their three children
as alien passengers, arriving at Ellis Island in 1903.

1

THE INHERITANCE WE DIED FOR

Freedom is never more than one generation away from extinction. We didn't pass it to our children in the bloodstream. It must be fought for, protected, and handed on for them to do the same, or one day we will spend our sunset years telling our children and our children's children what it was once like in the United States where men were free.

—RONALD REAGAN

Former President Reagan's weighty words reflect one side of the coin of our future. It is true that the cornerstone of our country—freedom—is always only one generation from extinction. And yet the other side of the coin is also true: America is only one generation from its greatest days.

What will make the difference?

Listening to today's predominant discourse will tell you that overhauled health care or free market solutions or reduced government spending will tip the scale. There are many theories about which matters most and many more theories about what the remedies must entail. Yet while these opportune topics must always be discussed, they should never steer the conversation. Such topics tend to focus resources on only the surface needs of some Americans without considering the substantive needs of every American. Our substantive needs are largely intangible, and intangibles are, unfortunately, easy to overlook.

However, the intangibles are topics we must never forget. They, and not the prevailing pundit drift, should dominate our discourse now and into the future. We need to remind ourselves of a time when this country's only ingredients were the gratitude, personal responsibility, and ongoing sacrifice of men and women who had taken great and sometimes grave risks for three very simple yet profound ideals: life, liberty, and the pursuit of happiness.

Our country's origin is defined by the characteristics of men and women who left their homes and livelihoods, the familiarity of their friends and the comforts of their native cultures, to pursue the promise of something better than the world had ever known. They were Europeans mostly, and among them members of my own family. My great-grandparents left everything they knew in Cerda, Sicily, to embark on a passenger boat for America with only the clothes on their backs and twenty dollars to their name. They were certainly not alone in their journey. Many others made the dangerous voyage too—at some point, members from most of our families did. I often wonder what filled their thoughts and what their conversations were like. One thing I know is that what dominated the discourse of their day should still dominate our discourse today, because theirs were not only the topics that unified the first Americans—they are the topics that drove the dawning of the American dynasty, one which, despite differences and disagreements, compelled us to care for one another and fight for one another.

Isn't this the America you believe in?

Isn't this the heritage you hope to leave to your children and grandchildren?

We are a country, yes. But we are more than that—like a family, we are bound together by a history and a heritage that includes a set of ideals, values, and principles that make us who we are and show us who we can become. To be certain, members of our country, like members of a family, don't always see eye to eye. But families remain together when their hearts remain united by their core principles, values, and standards. Such unity should be the driving force today, because Reagan is right—America's inheritance never was or will be passed down in the bloodstream. Yet it must be passed down, somehow, if we are to remain united like no other country in the world.

How that must happen is what this book is all about.

Do you believe the founding values of the United States of America are permanent and, to quote Shakespeare, "an ever-fixed mark [t]hat looks on tempests and is never shaken"?

This is the question at the root of the great and confusing complex of issues with which our nation is currently grappling. We can all agree that the Declaration of Independence, the Constitution of the United States, and the principles codified in them are the basis upon which this nation was founded. But should we stretch or alter our values in order to meet the challenges of our time or the prevailing cultural expectations?

America was founded—as John Adams said—on "the most stupendous articles" ever laid before a parliament of men. Those articles were based on the first principles of the rights of man and were so resilient and redeeming that even the most cynical examination of American history reflects a constant march toward a "more perfect union" by means of constant correction of wrongs.

Those founding values were responsible over time for the rise of an American dynasty that has been—though not without its mistakes—a constant force for good in the world, extending the benefits of liberty and prosperity to the largest number of people at any time in human history. America was made great through its founding values and exercised its greatness more in its generosity than in conquest or imposition.

But now America faces headwinds of ruthless partisanship, imperial overreach, and economic implosion.

Who among us—at least those who are honest and not blinded by aimless nationalism—would not admit that our nation has lost its way? Who will deny that the values that gave us the humane living we enjoy seem to have been forgotten? If our Founding Fathers could observe us today would gratitude, personal responsibility, and a willingness to sacrifice for the sake of national prosperity be evident? Who does not feel the threatening hand of fate and the collapsing favor of fortune warning us that if we are to survive and thrive as a nation we must return to what made us what we are? And who does not fear that things have run so far away from those values, that a system of corruption has now emerged in which our citizens and elected officials demonize rather than disagree, compromise rather than cooperate, and react rather than respond?

Our nation stands at a crossroads: Either we will recognize the forces that are pulling us farther and farther apart, and make the difficult choices and sacrifices necessary to rescue America, or we will lose the world's last great hope for humanity.

The solutions required will not be agreed upon easily or take effect immediately, but the urgency of our situation requires a radical refocusing on what has always been essential in the making of America. Make no mistake—we are in a fight for our survival. If we do not commit ourselves to rescue America, she will surely perish.

The problem with the current debate over what ails our nation is that it places effects in the position of causes. Those forces put forth as primary causes of our decline are actually large systems of effects driven within our political culture, effects that are so obvious, so tangible, that we come to regard them as more fundamental than they are.

There is no doubt, for instance, that departure from prudence in international affairs, resulting in expensive misadventures abroad over the last hundred years, is certainly a force in the nation's present state of affairs. Government spending has run amok, with successive administrations and Congress passing pork-laden legislation, each party with its own pet projects adding to our national financial burdens, and neither side having the credibility to speak for the prudence that was once the hallmark of American fiscal management. Who can doubt that our present economic woes owe as much to the orgiastic greed exhibited on Wall Street as to a dereliction of duty in Washington and to imprudence in the population in general?

Still others say the cause of our decline is the societal malaise, excesses, and debauchery of a people grown fat—literally—on profligate government entitlements.

Finally, there are those who argue that our decline is being authored by combinations of these factors, resulting in the decimation of our sense of national community, the disintegration of the family unit, and the decline of America. While this comes closest to the truth, the true cause of our problems is that we no longer create citizens who understand and embrace the core values that made this nation "the United States of America."

A zero sum game has been created in which the larger questions of the needs and health of the nation are overrun by those who routinely absolve themselves of personal responsibility, seeking immediate satisfaction and making demands on the nation that are inconsistent with its foundational values. As such, the causes for decline lie in the psychological evisceration of the ideals and practice of gratitude, personal responsibility, and sacrifice upon which the first Americans came together.

Our first duty, then, is to produce the kind of citizen capable of sustaining this nation's great heritage. We must produce this level of citizenship in ourselves and in those around us. We must cultivate citizens who understand what it means to "be American" and who instill in each subsequent generation, and in those immigrants we welcome to our shores, a culture that embraces and upholds a lifestyle of gratitude, personal responsibility, and sacrifice—a citizenry who feel a burning sense of gratitude for the opportunities provided by a nation built on the efforts and sacrifices of those who came before them; who take responsibility for themselves and for all the outcomes of their lives; and who are willing and determined to make further sacrifices to both seize the opportunities America offers and to perpetuate America's greatness.

It is true that at the very moment our Founding Fathers were announcing the values of such citizenry, the nation was committing atrocities (such as slavery) that violated the values themselves. Yet that fact does not make these values any less legitimate and worthy. We must simply look to the Preamble to the Constitution of the United States for guidance: "We the people of the United States, in order to form a more perfect union . . ." This means, among other things, that the people of America are—or should be—constantly perfecting this nation by admitting wrongs, correcting injustices, and making a sustained effort to protect, uphold, and solidify its foundation.

Consider the parents and grandparents of what Tom Brokaw has labeled the "Greatest Generation." Before 1900, these predecessors of America's Greatest Generation consisted primarily of generations of immigrants, mostly from Europe, who came to this country at great risk and embraced and adopted America's founding values. These would-be citizens didn't board 747s, sipping mimosas en route and landing seven hours later at JFK airport. They left their homes, the lands they knew, their neighbors and friends, and often their family—all the unspoken intimacies, certainties, and sinews of their histories—and traveled weeks, sometimes months, across the Atlantic knowing they might not ever reach the land of their dreams.

Why would they risk everything? It had to be for something truly extraordinary.

They came because of the appeal of the American Experiment, the draw of American values, the promise of a more perfect union. And when they landed, first and foremost among their instincts was a sincere feeling of gratitude—gratitude for the privilege of being in America and gratitude for the sacrifices made by so many to create this nation. They were motivated by a duty to work hard, to take responsibility for the outcomes of their lives (good or bad). And they were compelled to make further sacrifices as they embraced the opportunities America provided. The men and women of the Greatest Generation were heirs to this legacy.

Such heirs seem missing today. Has the legacy been damaged?

Yes. But not beyond repair. Still, that repair begins with you and me.

Dr. Martin Luther King Jr. is one who understood this. His deep philosophical insight into American values as our great moral teacher was inspiring. He believed so profoundly in those values that his life was spent advocating—and was even sacrificed—for the sort of change that moved us ever closer to a more perfect embodiment of them. With a magisterial eloquence—matched in our history, in my view, only by Abraham Lincoln—King prophesied, "I have a dream that one day this nation will rise up and live out the true meaning of its creed: 'We hold these truths to be self-evident, that all men are created equal.'"

This creed was for him, as it should be for all Americans, "an ever-fixed mark." Our rescue lies in a committed march toward a more perfect embodiment of the values that uphold such foundational creeds.

Citizens of most nations speak of a faith in their country. But given that America was initiated and built on values, it is much more appropriate to speak of a faith in "American values." At a clear and decisive point, the values by which we consented to live were established, and they were sufficiently broad and deep to allow us to grow as a nation. Those values—life, liberty, the pursuit of happiness—have produced such high levels of protection and prosperity that we honor those who have given the "last full measure of devotion"—ultimate sacrifices of life, liberty, and happiness—for them. We commemorate them because they demonstrate for us that it is possible to have faith in those values in an absolute way, beyond faith in the country itself.

To emphasize the difficulty and the quiet but stupendous majesty of this faith, I can say that it rests upon something all lovers of liberty feel instinctively: Justice, while often delayed, is not ultimately justice denied. Or as Dr. King once said: "The arc of the moral universe is long, but it bends toward justice." This is the same faith those like Frederick Douglass continued to hold despite being denied the benefits of liberty—whether because of racism, ideology, or expediency. These faithful did not define America or the strength of its values by that denial or delay. They believed the values upon which America was founded were larger, more powerful, and more evocative than the moment of their suffering. They believed justice would one day come.

Under and because of this faith, we have endured what no logic could convince us to endure. We hold fast, knowing these founding values make it possible for the greatest number of human beings to become their best selves, to experience life, liberty, and the pursuit of happiness.

1. I believe in American exceptionalism.
2. I believe in America, in the values upon which America was founded, and what it stands for. As I have seen the sacrifices made by the relative few, on behalf of so many, and as I have experienced firsthand great successes and painful failures, I have come to better understand the true magic and majesty of this great young nation. And through the good times and the bad, I have found honor and reward in simply entering the arena this nation provides, playing in this game of life and giving it my all. Here, as nowhere else, I can move with a resolve in the areas of my own interest, without fear that I will be in any other way impeded by law and without fear that what I reap from my own efforts will be taken from me.
3. I believe in America's founding values and the ethic upon which this nation was formed. I believe in an America that embodies and embraces a spirit of freedom, personal responsibility, and success through sacrifice. I am made humble by the sacrifices of many, including those in my own family, and I recommit myself to the ideals of this great country. Every day I am driven by my gratitude for the price that has been paid for the freedoms we all enjoy as American citizens.
4. I believe in an America that reconceived the notion of what it means to be a human being and a citizen. This nation gave meaning to the rule of law and has—in its short life—paid every price, borne every burden, and sacrificed its blood and treasure to give hope, freedom, and prosperity to nations around the world. America's generosity has brought means and hope to the darkest corners of the globe.

5. I believe in an America whose middle class enjoys a prosperity that far exceeds and outpaces that of all the nations of Western Europe combined. I believe in a nation that has produced the greatest wealth the world has ever known.

6. I believe in an America in which an immigrant with an eighth-grade education, who leaves his native land in search of opportunity, can make a successful and honorable life for himself and his family. I believe in a country that embraced and empowered my great-grandparents the moment they set foot on Ellis Island.

7. I believe in an America that has, along the way, made many mistakes and at times meted out injustices, and yet, in pursuit of a "more perfect union," still strives to uphold its founding values of life, liberty, and the pursuit of happiness, and to embody gratitude, personal responsibility, and sacrifice so that today, more than yesterday, people are truly—and increasingly—equal and free.

I fear that America has become not at all what the Founding Fathers had imagined. And if they were to arise as Rip van Winkle did, would they find favor and take pride in what had become of their blessed Experiment? Would they regard us as good stewards of the profound American Paradigm they and many others—even our sons and daughters, mothers, fathers, grandmothers, and grandfathers—fought and died to uphold? Would they believe the trials and tribulations had not been in vain?

It is time for each American to contribute again to the great American Experiment, to practice advanced citizenship, to move our country closer to a more perfect union. These activities are, after all, more than mere answers to a history exam. They are the air we, as American heirs, breathe.

To that end this book will explore what made America the "last best hope of earth," as Abraham Lincoln put it; when and why we declined from that position; and how we can rescue America from its current path and restore it to its greatness.

Rediscover the significance of our founding values through these pages, examine honestly your role in our great nation's decline, and be inspired to take part in its salvation. We have inherited much as Americans. In return, we should ensure that this inheritance continues.

Despite the litany of concerns, all is not lost for America. Charles Krauthammer, in his column for the *Weekly Standard*, said it best: "For America today, decline is not a condition. Decline is a choice."

What will we choose?

2

THE STANDARD WE STOOD FOR

The historic glory of America lies in the fact that it is the one nation that was founded like a church. That is, it was founded on a faith that was not merely summed up after it had existed; it was defined before it existed.

—G. K. CHESTERTON

America's great standard of equality, inalienable rights, and life, liberty, and the pursuit of happiness is the most profound and deliberate upon which any nation in human history was established. There is no greater or more perfect embodiment of this standard than human freedom. There are no rights greater than those endowed by our Creator. The power of the American Experiment is this: Every American is able to imagine any triumph and to bear any challenge because we are free. And because the nation was founded on such freedom, the living history of America is embodied in its constant and advancing manifestation of the values that support and protect it.

In fact, without such values, America is not possible. Without them, Americans have no basis for becoming a unified nation of people. We are but a cacophony of indecipherable voices claiming, demanding, and distorting the benefits of America without ever acting or sacrificing to maintain or advance them. Without them, the ideal captured in the Latin phrase *e pluribus unum*—out of many, one—would be unattainable.

In learning how to sustain our faith in what America stood for from the beginning, we must first understand the core values themselves and the principles with which they are enacted. We must develop a deep and flourishing awareness of the attractive power of the dawning American dynasty to act upon the imaginations of those who sought refuge on our shores, who validated the American Experiment not merely by their arrival here but by living out the American Dream.

AMERICA IS EXCEPTIONAL

Though it had its "birthing pains," America attempted to make an immediate and absolute commitment to human freedom from the moment of its conception. American values did not come into being by accident; they were the result of what is perhaps the most profound research experiment conducted by men concerned with the founding of a new citizenry. Ideals and models of government were imagined, proposed, and discarded. From other national experiments, philosophers, and kingdoms of old, the Founding Fathers extracted the best features and added them to a new structure and method that matured into an American Paradigm. It was the first, most deliberate establishment of a commonwealth of citizens in human history.

By comparison, the European political experience, in its march toward the liberty of mankind, was in constant tension with the imperial power of monarchy, which was supported by the authority of the Christian Church. Neither kings nor clergy had an interest in a government by, of, or for the people. The rise of liberty in Europe thus did not have a specific point at which all European nations accepted or adhered to the notion of human freedom. Nations moved incrementally toward liberty and democracy over centuries. Each new principle was advanced through confrontation, as with the challenging of the monarch's authority through the Magna Carta in 1215 and the Cromwellian revolt from 1642 to 1649. Each victory inched Europe closer and closer to democratic forms of government.

While Europe gave us language, certain cultural influences, and a host of unnameable features of nationhood and society, in matters of liberty and equality, America was deliberate and specific and is—in fact—exceptional in human history. There has never been a national paradigm like that established in 1776.

THE DECLARATION OF INDEPENDENCE

The Declaration of Independence was the catalyst that ignited a new American spirit, one that laid a foundation for the freedom and enterprise that led America to its prominence. The Declaration itself was, in profound respects, a letter to King George III informing him of the will and character of the new "American" peoples and the civic values that motivated their separation from him and his kingdom.

These principles would have seemed bizarre to most European sovereigns at that time in history. The only inalienable rights endowed by the Creator that they recognized were their own. Yet Thomas Jefferson, the primary author of the Declaration, was not the first promoter of such ideas. Most of the scholarly literature points to English philosophers as the main influence on Jefferson's thinking, but research reveals that he was also much influenced by French eighteenth-century philosopher Jean-Jacques Rousseau, whose commitment to the wisdom of citizens, called the "general will," is consistent with Jefferson's belief in government by the many rather than the few. Jefferson was likewise swayed by the thinkers of the English Enlightenment (principally John Locke and, to a lesser degree, Immanuel Kant), and more discreetly by Richard Cumberland, a philosopher of natural law, and Gottfried Wilhelm Leibniz, the true genius of continental philosophy and mathematics, whose logic seduced Jefferson.

What is not as well known is Jefferson's indebtedness to the Scottish Enlightenment, particularly Adam Smith's principles in *An Inquiry into the Causes of the Wealth of Nations*. That work was drawn both from Smith's own *Theory of the Moral Sentiments and Jurisprudence* and Thomas Reid's ideas in *Inquiry into the Human Mind on the Principles of Common Sense*. The Scots occupied an interesting position as a European people who had experienced subjugation and who possessed a Calvinistic "hard-headedness" and practicality that led to clear, unembellished principles. Commenting on Smith in a letter, Jefferson wrote, "In political economy I think Smith's *Wealth of Nations* the best book extant."[1] And in 1816 in a commentary on the *Treatise on Political Economy* by Destutt de Tracy, Jefferson wrote, "Adam Smith, first in England, published a rational and systematic work on Political economy, adopting generally the ground of the Economists, but differing on the subjects before specified. The system being novel, much argument and detail seemed then necessary to establish principles which now are assented to as soon as proposed."[2]

In fact, the following arguments in Smith's work underscore the core thesis in the Declaration of Independence:

> The natural effort of every individual to better his own condition, when suffered to exert itself with freedom and security, is so powerful a principle, that it is alone, and without any assistance, not only capable of carrying on the society to wealth and prosperity, but of surmounting a hundred impertinent obstructions with which the folly of human laws too often encumbers its operations.[3]

> *"The natural effort of every individual to better his own condition . . . is so powerful a principle . . . [it is] capable of carrying on the society to wealth and prosperity . . . [and] surmounting a hundred impertinent obstructions . . ."*
> —*Adam Smith*

Smith advocated government by, of, and for the people. That is, people who live in comfort and assurance of a government that protects these rights as its first duty, and who are then inspired to industry to advance their own interests and, as a result, the interests of their communities and their nation.

This is the underlying concept of the American Paradigm.

The Declaration was and is foundational, and reform that pulls us from the values within it is an attempt to turn America into something it is not and cannot be. The best way to understand this is to explore the values themselves.

SELF-EVIDENT TRUTHS

Imagine that a man says to you, "I am an uncle." Without knowing anything more, you could say with certainty that the man must have two of four relatives: a sister or a brother and a niece or a nephew. It cannot be doubted, cannot be disputed, and has no need of further explanation.

That is the nature of the "truths" laid out in the Declaration of Independence: They cannot be doubted, and to dispute them is to assault the self-evident truths of common sense.

What are those truths?

a. "That all men are created equal"
b. "That they are endowed by their Creator with certain unalienable rights"
c. "That among these are life, liberty, and the pursuit of happiness"

It is self-evident, wrote Jefferson, that all men are equal because God gave each individual an equal capacity for choice. This capacity for choice is the basis for our freedom and rights. (The distinction between the "capacity for choice" and the "freedom to choose" is described further in the subsections "Equality of Capacity" and "Equality Before the Law" later in this chapter.)

And these rights are inalienable. Not only can they not be taken away from the individual by a monarch or a politician or another human being, but individuals themselves cannot surrender or give them away. These rights include the right to life, to be free, and to pursue one's own happiness.

The Ideal of Equality in America

In the most famous phrase in the Declaration of Independence—"All men are created equal"—the technical term "equality" is never used, yet it is implied. Jefferson does not propose an ideal; he "recognizes" or acknowledges an equality that already exists, an equality with which the Creator endowed "all men."

In principle, Jeffersonian equality refers to a number of concepts that make up equality as an American ideal.

Equality of Value

If "all men" received the same "endowment" from the Creator, then all men are of equal value before that Creator. This value must be regarded, asserted, and protected by the sovereign or the state. Immanuel Kant proposed a famous principle called the "Categorical Imperative": "Act in such a way that you treat humanity, whether in your own person or in the person of any other, always at the same time as an end and never merely as a means to an end." This is, in some ways, a reformulation of Christ's admonition, "Do unto others as you would have them do unto you."[4] These two principles call upon us to use our need to be treated fairly and with dignity as a guide for the treatment of others. Yet Kant goes further, explicitly calling on us to treat ourselves as an end or as possessing inherent value, and to treat others likewise because we are equally valuable.

Equality of Capacity

Equality, for Jefferson, was not limited to inherent value endowed by our Creator. He also believed that central to that inherent value was a capacity that specifically characterizes human beings. Jefferson thought that to be a human being was to be a "choosing being." Therefore, the basis of morality, the basis of the principles of virtue, responsibility, diligence, and prudence, and the basis of independence is our capacity to choose. This capacity to choose is equal in all men since it is at the heart of what it means to be human.

Equality Before the Law

The notion in law that "justice is blind" implies that justice can make no distinctions among those who stand before it; all humanity is equally dealt with according to the rule of law. This operational equality was central to the thinking of the Founding Fathers. Their goal was to erect a commonwealth of laws, not of men, to rid the political imagination of the specter of men in secret, dark, and high places deciding on the fate of their fellow men without recourse to a universally applied set of principles and rules. Taken together, the three principles of equality presented above constitute Jefferson's notion of equality. And together they advanced a new thinking in the making of nations: The first two—equality of value and capacity—are endowments, and equality before the law is the operational principle by which the first two are constantly maintained.

Yet of all the principles advanced by Jefferson, equality has been the most controversial because however conceived, equality is a difficult concept to enact, since everyone has a personal view on the notion and function of equality. Moreover, principles applied to a living situation often become less than the sum of the whole. Wherever individualism is a guiding principle, as in America, the ideal and practice of equality can present a state of conflict. Equality can be interpreted as "sameness," yet individualism defies that idea. Some people may take it to mean they deserve an equal share of what others possess, even if they have not labored for it. But our American notion of equality is the opportunity to labor according to one's own desire for improvement and advancement, though it may not produce equal results. And once we have labored we have the equal protection of the law to preserve that for which we labored.

Equality based on sameness is not the American principle. And sameness in all things was never a goal for Jefferson or the Founding Fathers.

Any interpretation of the value of equality that goes beyond securing the endowments, attempting instead to guarantee equality of results or outcomes, is not in line with the principles upon which this country was founded.

In America, though not without its incidences of similar acquisitive habits, the primary means of wealth accumulation was and is to work for it, to earn it, or to invest it and receive returns on investment. This was and is a sea change from the means and methods of the old world. Since the individual is preserved against the state in America, naturally government is limited. As such, it falls to the individual to advance his interests or pursue his happiness accordingly as his talents and desires dictate. The outcome of this individual enterprise cannot be guaranteed in an American sense, because the state is legitimized by the individual and therefore cannot guarantee the success—however relative—of any individual at another's expense.

A notion of equality that attempts to ensure certain outcomes based on the actions of individuals, dispersing the resulting benefits without regard for effort or talent, would amount to a constant recalculation of equality based on the prevailing ideology of whoever is in power. An ideology that demands that every human being, regardless of his commitment to his own well-being, deserves certain benefits whether he exercises his freedom to attain them or his opportunities to exploit them, is repugnant to the Jeffersonian principles. Equality of outcomes is antithetical to what America has stood for since its beginning.

In establishing the nation, our Founding Fathers decided there was something more fundamental than the freedom to choose, and that was the equality of the capacity for choice. This is a subtle but critical distinction. In the capacity for choice, each man chooses according to his learning, experiences, and situation—his frame of reference.

Therefore, it could be possible, in a nation resting upon the mere freedom to choose, to limit some men and women by ranking them according to a judgment of what they would choose based on their frame of reference. For instance, those who are less educated might be allowed to vote only in certain elections. They are free to choose, but because they are not deemed equal in their capacity to choose, their rights are limited. But the Founding

Fathers—in their wisdom—saw this pitfall, and they opted for something more fundamental: They surmised that each person shall have the right to exercise his freedom based not upon what he chose to do with that freedom, but instead upon this human capacity to choose, in the first instance, and that his choices would be unlimited so long as they did not interfere with the freedom of other people.

In America, the quality of our choices is not to be judged by our governments but by a marketplace of ideas in open competition, where the individual is free to rise or fall, succeed or fail according to her ability and effort. Each person's rights are grounded in his capacity as a human being to choose according to his interests.

INALIENABLE RIGHTS

The notion of inalienable rights ("unalienable Rights" in the Declaration of Independence) is often misperceived. The concept is not intended simply as a limitation on government to deny rights. Rather, the phrase attempts to confirm that the citizen has rights so bound to him eternally he cannot even give them away. Because you are a human being, you possess these rights. It was Benjamin Franklin—in reflection on this—who said, famously, "Those who give up essential liberty to purchase a little temporary safety serve neither liberty nor safety." This, above all, is the great fountain of joy and magic in American citizenship. The inalienable rights for our citizens recognized within our nation have beckoned broken spirits from across our borders and across the oceans, people who were and are willing to bear every burden in order to receive the privileges of American citizenship.

Life

In America, government was instituted not to preserve the power of the government but to protect the rights of the people, the highest being the inalienable right to life. In its simplest terms, this right means that the government has no power over the life and death of an individual without recourse to law. In monarchies and various other forms of government, the sovereign power had, in its grasp, a power over life and death, more often than not on a whim. In America, no such power was or is available.

Liberty

Jean-Jacques Rousseau wrote, "Man is born free, but everywhere is in chains." Jefferson similarly believed that liberty, like other rights, was a natural right, as did Rousseau. He also believed liberty was "endowed by the Creator."

Yet liberty, in practical terms in a functioning society, is and must be limited by the liberty of others. At times, any American's liberty may be limited by government's attempts to protect this right for others, for which, according to our law, the government must give reasons. But as Jefferson argued, the "balance of Liberty" in a society should only be limited insofar as it interferes with the liberty of others. This is meant to place government under a burden of justification wherever the liberty of the individual is impaired or suffers interference.

By comparison, Madisonian Liberty—or liberty as defined by any Federalist—includes both a limitation imposed by the liberty of others and a limitation imposed by the demands of the state. But this latter consideration, when thought through deeply enough, means that any state or sovereign interest that curtails liberty comes face-to-face with inalienability. The power and privileges of the state are not inalienable; they are conferred onto it by its citizens and thus cannot override the inalienable rights of the citizens.

The Pursuit of Happiness

Some people become very excited when they read that the pursuit of happiness is an inalienable right; they conclude it refers to personal happiness. Others believe the pursuit, not the end result, of happiness is what's protected. Both interpretations are incomplete.

The happiness Jefferson refers to is not of the "doing whatever I please, when it pleases me" variety. Rather, in America the inalienable right of the pursuit of happiness guarantees that one is free to become the best self that one is capable of becoming.

The concept of happiness or the consistent pursuit of happiness as a critical element of the life of an individual was not a new philosophy when Jefferson introduced it into the Declaration of Independence. Confucius captured it in the Doctrine of the Mean, espousing the lifelong pursuit of the balance between extremes, through which one finds happiness. Like the American values, this pursuit required diligence, prudence, responsibility, and forthrightness.

Aristotle wrote, "He is happy who lives in accordance with complete virtue and is sufficiently equipped with external goods, not for some chance period but throughout a complete life." These sentiments imply that "happiness" proceeds from a certain type of living, which he described as the function of man:

> The function of man is to live a certain kind of life, and this activity implies a rational principle, and the function of a good man is the good and noble performance of these, and If any action is well performed it is performed in accord with the appropriate excellence: If this is the case, then happiness turns out to be an activity of the soul in accordance with virtue.[5]

In his book on Jefferson and the Declaration of Independence, *Inventing America* (Mariner Books, 2002), Garry Wills writes: "Within its original rich context, the pursuit of happiness is a phenomenon both obvious and paradoxical. It supplies us with the ground of human right and the goal of human virtue. It is the basic drive of the self, and the only means given for transcending the self."

It is possible to attain the highest heights of philosophical obscurity on this issue. But for the sake of simplicity, the pursuit of happiness as Jefferson presented it calls for a republic of virtue: Where citizenship is concerned, Americans take their values from founding principles and not from family connections or cultural traditions. Those principles—life, liberty, and the pursuit of happiness—demand a constant pursuit of one's best self. And Jefferson's aim in the Declaration was to cultivate a commonwealth in which each citizen would have the opportunity to pursue his best self and in which as many of these "best selves" as possible could be realized.

THE AMERICAN PARADIGM

All of this discussion about equality and inalienable rights puts a strong focus on the individual, and promotion of individualism was certainly in the forefront of the minds of the Founding Fathers. But the phrase that comes directly after life, liberty, and the pursuit of happiness in the Declaration of Independence reorients us to its other primary goal: "That to secure these rights, Governments are instituted among Men, deriving their just Powers from the consent of the governed." They were envisioning a new form of government, one that was formed to protect the rights of its citizens but would also function through the consent of its citizens.

Fundamental to this new American Paradigm was a significant departure from the traditional function and purpose of law. In Europe, laws were established to protect the monarch and the crown's wealth and power, as well as to limit the rights of the individual. America, on the other hand, was founded and laws were created to protect the individual and to limit the power and reach of the government, not to secure power for those who govern.

The influence of Rousseau is evident in these ideas; his notion that a "just government derives its legitimacy from the consent of the governed" found a home in Jefferson's thoughts. Once the Founding Fathers had established the protected rights and the values upon which the nation would stand, they had to address the nature of the union they were envisioning to further those values.

By stating that the government we would eventually form would rule by the consent of its citizens, the Founding Fathers were not putting the responsibility for proper operation on the government itself. They put the responsibility on the citizens—in practical terms, those Americans who, in the grip of patriotism and desiring to show their commitment to "putting their nation first," claim they will give up rights in exchange for security risk, and to some extent abandon, both. It is impossible to relinquish your inalienable rights, just as it is impossible to relinquish your responsibility as a citizen to further the values upon which this nation was founded. Recall Franklin's warning: "Those who give up essential liberty to purchase a little temporary safety serve neither liberty nor safety."

Our values are unifying, one leading to the others, and vice versa. They are transitive, eternal, and self-generating; they are kept real in the attitudes and actions of citizens, not through the dictates of sovereigns or executive government. The Preamble to the United States Constitution testifies to the truth of these affirmations:

We the People of the United States, in Order to form a more perfect Union, establish Justice, insure domestic Tranquility, provide for the common defense, promote the general Welfare, and secure the Blessings of Liberty to ourselves and our Posterity, do ordain and establish this Constitution for the United States of America.

Ours is a government of the people, and the people ordain, or establish, a union based on the values that were the foundation of the country. That leads us to a clear picture of the American Paradigm.

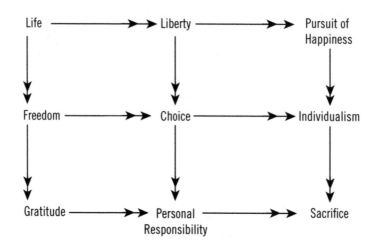

Figure 2.1—The American Paradigm

Altogether, the above graphic captures the meaning and the function of what it means to be an American. You may replace the words with similar ones. But once you begin with the founding values in the Declaration of Independence—life, liberty, and the pursuit of happiness—they lead inexorably to the principles of freedom, choice, and individualism. These values and principles, in turn, require a driving mechanism and so lead necessarily to the central activities of gratitude, personal responsibility, and sacrifice. Government's role is to act within this paradigm to protect these basic rights, leaving citizens free to seek out and exploit opportunities to become their best selves, wherever they are found and however they are cultivated, subject to law. Moreover, each citizen's role is to perpetuate the American Paradigm through this driving mechanism of gratitude, personal responsibility, and sacrifice.

GRATITUDE, PERSONAL RESPONSIBILITY, AND SACRIFICE

The American citizen can demand protection of his inalienable rights by his government. However, the bestowal of rights and demand for them is not the limit of the unifying properties of the American values. Without gratitude, there could be no appreciation for the sacrifices that brought us the life and liberties we enjoy, and thus no means of linking the past to the present, which would cause our grand experiment to lose both steam and focus. Without responsibility, there could be no government, given that the government operates by each citizen's consent, which as Rousseau argued is a responsibility that requires participation. Without sacrifice, there would be no vigilance against countervalues and habits of indulgence, nor would there be a means of sustaining the grand American Experiment by challenging the excesses and incongruities that can grow up around a nation founded on individualism and personal responsibility.

The practical aspect of being an American calls for a constant vigilance against selfish hysteria that promotes American life as a win-lose proposition; against an America dominated by the few at the expense of the many or where government seduces the many by taxing the few; and against an America where the protection of laws is broken and the values and principles of the American Paradigm become unsustainable.

If we fail at the self-regulation that sustains open societies, turn the ideal of American values into just an opportunity to express opinions rather than an obligation to assume duties, or perceive the American experience as little more than the right to receive the benefits of America without the responsibilities of being an American, our grand experiment will fail.

> *If we fail at the self-regulation that sustains open societies, turn the ideal of American values into just an opportunity to express opinions ... or perceive the American experience as little more than the right to receive the benefits of America without the responsibilities ... our grand experiment will fail.*

This is not a call for less individual competitiveness or for a withdrawal from acting in one's best interests or for self-sacrifice without profit. It is a wasteful and indulgent citizenry that forgets the values that brought their country into being while hoarding the very benefits those values make possible.

In his Gettysburg Address, Abraham Lincoln raised the meaning of the Civil War to an enterprise to preserve and advance the American Paradigm in a universal way:

It is rather for us to be here dedicated to the great task remaining before us—that from these honored dead we take increased devotion to that cause for which they gave the last full measure of devotion—that we here highly resolve that these dead shall not have died in vain—that this nation, under God, shall have a new birth of freedom—and that government of the people, by the people, for the people, shall not perish from the earth.

By this resolve, Lincoln has taught us, "We shall nobly save, or meanly lose, the last best hope of earth."

BEING AMERICAN, LIVING THE PARADIGM

E pluribus unum (latin for "out of many, one") is the motto that appears on the seal of the United States. It implies and asserts that the American nation is made up of a cornucopia of cultures. Under this country's founding principles, the many become one merely by accepting the values and principles themselves. The motto captures the willingness and intention to absorb other peoples into America's national identity.

In contrast, it is inconceivable for a foreigner to "become" English or French or Latvian. In such places, the new citizen has the task of adopting a culture that is hundreds, perhaps even thousands, of years old, and the individual also battles a lack of lineage that guarantees that one is English or French or Latvian. In America, because we are a country founded on a paradigm of values, principles, and actions, the new citizen adopts this paradigm and instantly becomes part of the American family and thus an heir to all our country represents. Our lineage, and therefore the inheritance we both received and pass down to future generations, is bound up in the constant translation of life, liberty, and the pursuit of happiness into the embodiment of gratitude, personal responsibility, and sacrifice.

We are unique as a nation in that we, like a family, are a unity of differences, and our commitment to choice, liberty, opportunity, and protection of laws is the source of our greatness.

The dedication of all citizens—whether by birth or naturalization—to this central endeavor is necessary for America's continued strength. We are unique as a nation in that we, like a family, are a unity of differences, and our commitment to choice, liberty, opportunity, and protection of laws is the source of our greatness. To ensure it continues, America must constantly produce Americans who (1) are aware of and grateful for the sacrifices that made them free; (2) possess a full sense of personal responsibility and individualism; and (3) regularly demonstrate a willingness to sacrifice for the sake of our American inheritance. Only when this activity is transferred to and sustained between generations will it cultivate a renewal of the foundational American spirit. Only this spirit, shared throughout our great land, will permit us to bequeath the security and prosperity we still enjoy. That is to say, the standard on which we originally stood will remain only if we make it stand.

> *Our lineage, and therefore the inheritance we both received and pass down to future generations, is bound up in the constant translation of life, liberty, and the pursuit of happiness into the embodiment of gratitude, personal responsibility, and sacrifice.*

3

THE FUTURE WE FOUGHT FOR

We ought not look back unless it is to derive useful lessons from past errors, and for the purpose of profiting by dearly bought experience.

—George Washington

America is not perfect. We know that because inherent in the foundation of America was a commitment to creating a "more perfect union." Both at and since its founding, America has made mistakes. Sometimes they've been egregious ones that cause suffering for others. It would be nonsense to deny this. No nation facing the crucial choices our country has faced, with the fate of billions of people in the balance, can exercise power without inflicting some pain. However, when one considers the nations of the world and their roles and impacts in human history, one cannot doubt American aims and ideals. Even when America's actions depart from those aims and ideals, it is in America, more so than in any other country, where that departure and the correction of a misguided course can gain a credible audience—where the country's actions can be criticized or protested by its citizens and whereby, in the form of its elections, those who have taken the country down a misguided course can be removed from power.

What country in the history of the world boasts a more impressive record of bettering the lot of all humanity than America? We can safely say none.

The Founding Fathers' belief in our inalienable rights of life, liberty, and the pursuit of happiness, with an acknowledgment of our inherent capacity to choose, gave birth to a creative and entrepreneurial spirit in this country. Furthermore, they believed this spirit to be inherent in all men, who needed only a government that recognized and guaranteed it. It unleashed the peculiar and particular talents of different persons from which we have gained advances in moral, economic, technological, and political thinking that could not have come from people whose thoughts and opportunities were directed by a governmental overlord.

The individual's belief in the American Paradigm and willingness to use that right of choice to assume risks in a competitive environment fostered this greatness. The magic of the American principles gave us genius, innovation, and courage that have made our national experience unique among nations. American values cultivate a certain dynamism based upon the exploits of this country's individual citizens, which is unprecedented for any other nation in the history of the world. This is the future our Founders sought in the beginning. It is the future our forefathers and grandfathers fought for time and again—with not only weapons of war but also weapons of will, wit, and resilience. This same future they envisioned and for which they risked so greatly is at risk today—if we do not learn the lessons of our legacy. This legacy begins, as it always has, with introspection and self-actualization. History proves the results.

The limitlessness of the human capacity to pursue one's best self unleashed a creativity that saw our nation find its footing against the English in 1776 and again in 1812. It saw us erect a constitutional system that secured our liberties against the state and between each other. It brought us through the Civil War into nationhood based on applied liberty for all. It saw the first rise of our economic dominance in the dawn of American industry. It saw us through the First World War and then through the Second World War, in which we liberated those who once held us bound. In intervening years, it opened us to the lessons of economic management and saw us through a Great Depression. It gave voice to civil rights and unleashed the postwar economic expansion that saw us become a force for good in the world. It defeated infectious diseases, placed a man on the moon, and gave us advanced communications technologies that now link the entire world in a global conversation through which we learn every day of the yearning of nearly forgotten peoples for the values of which we speak.

Our notions of and commitments to life, liberty, and the pursuit of happiness have become the aspiration of nations far and wide and the inspiration of all those who claim citizenship here.

THE LINCOLN PROPOSITION: THE LAND OF OPPORTUNITY

What drove the great creative and industrious spirit that produced growth and development here at home and American generosity abroad? For this we must turn to the great teacher among American presidents.

Abraham Lincoln gave expression to the framework of the American Experiment in a subtle yet profound way. Through his public discourse, he defined the role of individual industry as central to the definition of what it means to be an American. In a speech in Hartford, Connecticut, on March 5, 1860, he said: "God gave man a mouth to receive bread, hands to feed it, and the hand has a right to carry bread to his mouth without controversy . . . The ant, who has toiled and dragged a crumb to his nest, will furiously defend the fruit of his labor, against whatever robber assails him."

Lincoln gave voice to the distinctive American impulse. A new kind of ownership extended from the founding values of his relatively new nation: the ownership of the results of one's own industry, an ownership so natural and permanent that, unlike in other nations, a man could defend the fruits of his labor "without controversy."

In other nations, caste and class systems determined an individual's fate. No matter how bright, talented, or determined, a man found himself frozen in a particular standard of living, with a particular quality of life, with no hope of ever escaping the conditions into which he was born. In essence, those conditions came to define how his life would unfold from the cradle to the grave. Lincoln was not a social theorist or a philosopher. However, his statement of the practical operation of the American principle of individuality cannot be improved upon for its depth, philosophical consistency, practical efficiency, moral efficacy, and, more important, its attainability by all who seek it.

In 1856, reflecting deeply on this question—as was his habit—Lincoln said, "The man who labored for another last year, this year labors for himself, and next year he will hire others to work for him."[6] I refer to this as the "Lincoln Proposition." It is the most singular expression of Lincoln's vision of America.

The benefits Lincoln envisioned were conferred not by birthright or legal mandate but by the capacity and freedom to choose, by the quality of one's decisions, and by the inherent value and ownership of the fruit of one's labors. While we inherit the rights to such benefits from God-given freedom itself, the application of this inheritance is up to each individual. Obviously the

> *"The man who labored for another last year, this year labors for himself, and next year he will hire others to work for him."*
> —*Abraham Lincoln*

quality of our choices is not the same. Therefore the continuation of our great inheritance to the next generations depends upon the Lincoln Proposition being embraced by the majority of Americans.

Extrapolating from Lincoln's "man who labored for another last year," even if the person whom the man worked for inherited his money, still he contributes to the American Paradigm by creating jobs and opportunity. And that man who works for another must be driven by a uniquely American ambition. Lincoln envisioned the best of the new American spirit: not a man who works grudgingly or resentfully, but who works ambitiously because he is entitled to—and his government is mandated to protect—everything he works for. And he can expect, demand, and defend the fruits of his labor against all who might try to deny him those benefits. He knows, too, that his effort and commitment, and the pride he takes in his work, are his choice and will be credited to him as an individual.

The man who labors for another is confident that, with perseverance and applied imagination, he can, if he chooses, come to own the means of production, exceed the confines of laboring for another, and begin to labor for himself. This transition between working for others and working for oneself has been and continues to be easier in America than anywhere else in the world.

And now the man who once labored for others invites others to labor for him. He is imbued with and invested in—literally—the American spirit. This idea is a form of undirected, unmanaged, natural equality born of the American notion of opportunity for all; it is an idea driven by the individualism and ambition of those who determine for themselves to take risks and to reap the rewards. This equality of opportunity has offered and produced more rewards for the individual willing to apply himself than was ever offered by any other nation.

The American Dream that Lincoln defined was marked by an absence of jealousy, envy, and resentment in the social transaction of work and wealth in America. The attitude of the working man, one of personal responsibility, tells us something about the nation in which such a man lives. In that country, a man may take a job and discover and hone his talents by learning a skill from another who preceded him. The man who hired him does not regard him or the skill he learned as a possession to which the man who hires has an absolute right. Both men have an equal capacity to choose, and even though, for a time, their choices may have resulted in one man working for the other, the working man has no limits on his choices and one day may leave, replace, join, or supersede the man who hired him.

This opportunity to make of one's life what one chooses is the essence of dynamism that led to American greatness. And so, immigrants from the meanest, most horrific, and most soul-destroying nations on Earth readily and easily adopt this American spirit as soon as—at long last—their feet grace American soil.

AMERICA'S ECONOMIC PROWESS

Industry alone does not determine the greatness of a nation. Nor does it indicate that such a nation has achieved something in its principle of citizenship that can or should be embraced by everyone. After all, the Nazis made many infrastructural improvements in Germany, but we would embrace neither their approach to life or governance nor their values. Yet, while industry, individual or otherwise, is not the sole determinant of a nation's greatness, continued economic prosperity does speak to the opportunities provided to a nation's citizens and their willingness to partake of them. We may say for America that in making economic opportunity a routine process in the life of the individual, together with legal protections for what that opportunity yields by dint of application and prudent labor, two realities are revealed: First, American values are sustainable and have the capacity to unleash the limitless potential and productivity of mankind. Second, the American Experiment has been unprecedented in economic terms.

If you combined the wealth of the Greek, Roman, Chinese, and English empires, the wealth generated in America over the recent century would supersede them. The economic power of the United States was and is unmatched by any other country in the world. By every measure conceivable, the United States outpaced every nation and civilization in human history, in real as well as relative terms, in a variety of categories, but most notably in the provision of opportunity and wealth. (See the box titled "Our Vital Statistics" that follows.)

The reason for this is understandable: It is confidence, both domestically and internationally, in the American principles of the protection of private property and the promotion of opportunity—each as a result of the inalienable rights of life, liberty, and the pursuit of happiness.

American economic power is manifested as the power to create wealth, to provide opportunities, to generate wealth for and promote wealth generation in other nations, and to apply that wealth through the process and practice of American generosity. How have these principles resulted in such success in wealth creation for so many here and around the globe? Our principles drove the United States to attain the highest output and labor productivity in the world. That achievement is partly the result of a year's work for the average American increasing by 199 hours (about 3.8 hours per week) between 1973 and 2003. In 2008, America led the world in productivity per hour, overtaking Norway, France, Belgium, and Luxembourg, which had surpassed the United States for most of the preceding decade.[7] Without the incentives and opportunities the American economic system provides, this productivity would not be present, and it could not have occurred. If Americans felt that the results of their labor, of their choice to engage in the economic system, would not be protected by our political and legal system, their faith in the American economic system would not be maintained.

The power and flexibility of the U.S. labor markets translate into an adaptive economic and social system that promotes and reflects the freedom of the individuals within that system. Despite the presence of robust unions, the World Bank "ranks the United States first in the ease of hiring and firing workers."[8] There is an openness and comparative lack of encumbrance in the labor market in America that allows those who hire others to easily adjust as their needs change, to make the best choices to ensure both their survival and their ability to provide continued opportunities in the future. This is a proposition that is nearly impossible in Europe because of the prevalence and the power of its labor unions. Of course, recent events involving the National Labor Relations Board's suit to prevent Boeing, our nation's largest exporter, from locating its new manufacturing plant in South Carolina may change this ranking in the future if the verdict does not reflect our freedoms.

OUR VITAL STATISTICS

As expressed by the International Monetary Fund, the U.S. gross domestic product (GDP) is measured at $14.4 trillion dollars. That amounts to 23.9 percent of total production in the world.

It takes thirty two nations in the European Union to match U.S. GDP.

In terms of total GDP, China is the second largest, at $7.99 trillion, and Japan is third, at $4.3 trillion.

In terms of concentrations of global wealth, 50 percent of the world's five hundred billionaires and 32 percent of the world's 25 million millionaires are Americans. The United States attained the benchmark of 7 million people worth at least $7 million dollars near the end of the twentieth century.

Over 70 percent of global savings are held in the United States. There are only about five nations in the world in which one's money is safe from government intrusion. Among them, the United States leads in global banking confidence, where the concern is safekeeping of financial assets. The world shows its vote of confidence by the placement of portfolio capital into the U.S. banking system, which in 2009 amounted to more than $330 billion dollars. In total, foreign investment in the United States—including funds under management—totals over $35.5 trillion dollars of the $111.5 trillion under management globally.

Fifty percent of the world's largest companies are in the United States, as are nearly 50 percent of the world's largest and most important banks. The United States is home to the world's largest retailer, largest oil company, largest telecommunications company, and largest software company.

Eighteen of the top twenty universities are in the United States, and eight of the top ten research centers call America home.

Foreign direct investment (FDI) is the measure of foreign investment in the long-term ownership or management of an enterprise or productive asset in another country. In this area the United States has been the most favored nation in the world, with FDI reaching $325 billion in 2008. That number fell in 2009 to $135 billion due largely to fears about the economic and financial crisis. Interestingly, however, portfolio investments (i.e., investments in U.S. government bonds, securities, and savings deposits) increased significantly during the financial crisis, as America remained the most trusted financial system in the world. Today, approximately 70 percent of global savings is held in the United States.

The United States is the third largest producer of oil in the world as well as its largest importer. It is the world's number one producer of electrical and nuclear energy and liquid natural gas.

The other critical component to the success of our economic system is that, while there are clear challenges to reining in federal government spending, the U.S. economy is comparatively private, which is in keeping with its founding values of providing opportunities for the individual and protecting the resulting benefits. For instance, in 2009 the private sector in the United States constituted nearly 54 percent of U.S. economic activity, with the federal government speaking for just over 22 percent and the states and municipalities representing just under 20 percent. Of course, the somewhat limited role of the government can be called into question with the 2009 takeover of General Motors, where the interests of senior bondholders (lenders with contractual rights) were wiped out in favor of giving an ownership interest to the unions. Though common in Europe, Asia, and South America, this type of action on the part of the government is a dramatic divergence from the fundamental principle of property rights in the United States.

Laws, policies, and social and political initiatives in America were designed by our founders to limit the government and protect the governed. This distinctive philosophy has produced—among other things—a stupendous prosperity driven by individuals acting in their own best self-interest and taking personal responsibility for the outcomes of their own lives.

AMERICAN GENEROSITY

While our economic statistics reveal America's power to provide an unmatched standard of living and quality of life for its citizens, they do not tell the entire story. Another equally unmatched and yet more compelling story is the application of the wealth created for the good of billions around the world. "To whom much is given, much is required," was first pronounced by Jesus and then reiterated by John F. Kennedy.[9] America's greatness in responding to that responsibility—though largely unacknowledged, even by Americans—cannot be doubted. If Winston Churchill is right that "we make a living by what we get and make a life by what we give," then what we call America's "greatness" should be celebrated even by those who are not citizens of this country.

Our generosity is a direct result of our economic vigor. One can draw a distinct parallel to the biblical story of the Good Samaritan. The generosity that is central to the story is possible because the Samaritan was a man of means. Had he not been, he may still have stopped to help the wounded man, but he would not have had wine and olive oil to treat the wounds, would not have had a donkey on which to carry the wounded man to safety, and would not have had the money to put him up at the inn and promise to pay the inn-keeper for all of his expenses. The Samaritan had a generous spirit, and even those of humble means can exhibit generosity every day. But in addition to his compassion, kindness, generosity, and good faith, he also had the means and/or stature to follow through on his intentions.

We have discussed how the American definition of the term human being is a person with the capacity to choose; it is the basis of American humanity as reflected in our founding documents. It is this principle that America seeks to protect in its best efforts abroad. America as a nation and Americans as individuals have chosen to protect those who claim our nation is belligerent, to feed those who accuse our nation of materialism, and to protect the wealth of those who claim our nation is untrustworthy.

The generosity of Americans—to a degree unprecedented in human history—was on display most recently during the Haitian crisis stemming from an earthquake in January 2010. Some will say that the United States played a role in Haiti's history of displacement and searing poverty, that Haiti was used as a pawn in the geopolitics of countries near our shores. There may be some truth to that. It would be foolish and intellectually dishonest to pretend such things do not occur. But unlike so many other nations, America is built on underlying principles that enable it to constantly return to the ethics of its founding values—its origin—and make of a mistake something noble and ennobling. In the case of Haiti, during a recent Senate Foreign Relations Committee hearing, government officials cautioned that this time we must ensure Haiti's resurgence according to the first principles of natural rights and human dignity and in terms that will lead to prosperity based on individual initiative and personal responsibility. This is what Benjamin Disraeli meant when he famously asserted, "The greatest good you can do for another is not just to share your riches but to reveal to him his own."

REMITTANCES: AMERICA'S STEALTH GENEROSITY

Across the world and over the years, immigrants from almost every nation—no matter how prosperous—have come to our shores seeking the American Dream. It turns out that those who arrive in America and thrive under our values and our definition of a human being produce an astounding impact on their home countries through the export of American cash in the form of remittances. In a study on remittances in 2004, the Inter-American Development Bank reported these critical and useful insights: "Sixty percent of the 16.5 million Latin American–born immigrants residing in the United States engaged in remittance transactions, generating over 100 million individual transactions per year, or an estimated $30 billion during 2004."[10] While the remittances sent back to their countries averaged between 10 and 11 percent of their total household income in America, it amounted to 50 to 80 percent of the household incomes for the recipients in their countries of origin. Participation in this enterprise is drawn from almost every corner of the United States, as the largest remittances were sent from thirty-seven of the fifty states.

In the Caribbean, U.S.-originated remittances equal 13 percent of total GDP, according to the World Bank. Mexico alone takes in 38 percent of the total remittances in the region, at a little over $20 billion a year (2.8 percent of GDP). Brazil, with 12 percent, takes in $6 billion (1.1 percent of GDP), followed by Colombia, with 6 percent, at $3 billion a year (3.3 percent of GDP). In fact, the impact of remittances from the United States outpaces FDI and all other financial assistance to those countries.

Driven by an open market system and free individuals acting in their own interests, remittances reveal the power and impact of our American values outside of our borders.

THE WORLD'S SECURITY BLANKET

As a force for good, America's generosity extends beyond financial assistance to geopolitical obligations of enormous consequences.

In 1998 and 1999, for example, the United States stepped into an ethnic morass during the disintegration of what used to be Yugoslavia. After months of drift and indecision by European governments, the United States led its NATO partners into collective action to end escalating violence that had by that point opened up on three fronts, with the indiscriminate killing of civilians—including women and children—on all sides. The U.S.-led operation included a 78-day NATO bombing campaign (Operation Allied Force) against Serbian positions until Yugoslavian leader Slobodan Milosevic, who had exacted a hellish toll on people Serbians had once called neighbors, withdrew his forces.

Although this was primarily a European conflict, the United States has committed peacekeeping troops to Kosovo since 1999, and it committed to support—at its own expense—a continuing military presence in the conflict theater until well past a political settlement was reached that included Kosovo independence. A 2008 Congressional Research Service Report demonstrates how the U.S. role in Kosovo reflects this nation's larger role in the world. Without intending to, the report shows how America's role evolves, even when it attempts to take merely a support position.

> Over the years, U.S. engagement in Kosovo has at times been controversial. Proponents of U.S. engagement say that instability in Kosovo could have a negative impact on the stability of the Balkans and therefore of Europe as a whole . . . could produce an environment favorable to organized crime and terrorism and undermine U.S. goals of Euro-Atlantic integration and cooperation. They say the ongoing involvement of the United States is critical to ensuring this stability, because of its resources and unrivaled political credibility in the region.
>
> Increasingly, many observers on both sides of the Atlantic emphasize that Europe has a larger stake than the United States in stability in southeastern Europe, and that European nations should lead international efforts in Kosovo. Some critics of U.S. engagement in the Balkans say that the situation in Kosovo does not have as large an impact on vital U.S. interests as other issues, particularly the war on terrorism in the wake of the September 11 terrorist attacks on the United States and the war in Iraq, as well as a host of other foreign policy and national security challenges. Reflecting international focus on the global anti-terrorism campaign and other priorities, there has appeared a strong interest in "finishing the job," including an eventual "exit strategy" for the international civil and military administration of Kosovo. However, a residual international civilian and military role, with an ongoing NATO and U.S. presence—including an ongoing commitment of U.S. resources—is likely to stay on for some time after independence to assist with and supervise Kosovo's transition.[11]

The report emphasizes the disproportionate demands for U.S. support and all it entails, and how this shapes the long-term commitment of U.S. resources for the protection of quite wealthy nations—at nearly no cost to themselves. If nothing else, this report reflects the attitudes, actions, and commitments of so much of the rest of the world: The United States is expected to be the self-financed default bearer of burdens for peace and safety. Yet, and strangely, the United States is left to bear the criticism when things—as they always will—go wrong.

Even in the face of these attitudes, however, the American people are the first—as they were during the Iranian earthquake in 2005—to offer their assistance.

THE MARSHALL PLAN

With the application of our resources of blood and treasure, the United States has maintained the safety and financial stability of Europe since the Second World War. During and after that time of warfare, America's power to generate wealth and employ that wealth for good was exhibited in the greatest display of economic comity from one nation to others in human history. Within two years of the war's end, the United States instituted the Marshall Plan, or European Recovery Program, acting as a leader of the free world on a grand scale for the first time. The Marshall Plan's primary intent was European economic recovery and stability. But more than that, through the introduction of American values and principles (including drafting the constitutions of several of its former enemies), it set a direction for the development of European markets that ensured the prolonged prosperity of the people of those countries—at American expense and driven by American ingenuity.

In the mid-1940s in Europe, most of the industry on the continent lay in ruins, and some have argued that the United States undertook the Marshall Plan merely to restore markets in Europe for American industry. The truth, however, is that the passage of the plan not only prevented the collapse of the Western coalition but also imposed upon Europe a discipline forcing it to abandon old socialistic policies and to introduce open market systems. The Marshall Plan played a key role in inaugurating the postwar era of prosperity and political stability in Western Europe, and it significantly sped Western European growth by altering the environment in which economic policy was made.

In the immediate aftermath of the Second World War, politicians who recalled the disasters of the Great Depression were ill disposed to trust the stock market and were eager to embrace regulation and government control. Had European political economy taken a different turn, centralized planning and the use of laws and regulations to limit individuals and markets might have hobbled postwar recovery. Instead, intervention by the United States in the postwar reconstruction of Europe forced liberalization and dismantling of controls over economic market processes. The Marshall Plan era saw the restoration of price and exchange rate stability, and Marshall Plan aid gave governments room to maneuver in order to carry out their intentions. Consequently, Europe returned to growth and stability long before anyone expected.

European billionaires or millionaires, as well as every European household, enjoy prosperity today not just because of what the Marshall Plan achieved but also because the American taxpayer continues to underwrite their safety and security—without complaint, controversy, or reimbursement.

TWO LETTERS OF GRATITUDE TO AMERICA

Though the demands on American generosity are great and the repercussions can be less than positive, gratitude for American generosity and values does exist. Regrettably, however, we have not seen it in proportional supply at home or abroad.

Helmut Schmidt was Chancellor of West Germany from 1974 to 1982. In a letter he wrote in July 2007 to the *Atlantic Times*, he made references to the Marshall Plan and explained how American generosity rebuilt his country after it was defeated as the aggressor in the Second World War. Here is an excerpt from his letter:

"I Believe in America," by Helmut Schmidt

My first visit to the U.S. was in 1950, when I had to represent the port of my home city of Hamburg during an international trade fair at the navy pier in Chicago. It happened to be a very poor show as far as Hamburg was concerned. Our port was 100 percent destroyed and full of wrecked ships; and all I could offer were plans and papers for a reconstruction that in fact had not started as yet. But I was full of optimism because the U.S. had already started its European Recovery Program, the Marshall Plan. And to the great relief of us Germans, the U.S. already had graciously included our defeated country into that great recovery program.

I was amazed at this generosity. During the war I had foreseen us Germans living in holes in the earth; and never had I hoped for much help from the victorious Americans. But now, in the summer of 1950, after eight years of service as a drafted soldier and after three years of rather superficial studies at a destroyed university, already 31 years old but still only in my first year in an ordinary paid job, I came to see America and experience its vitality. I was overwhelmed.[12]

In 1973, Mr. Gordon Sinclair, a respected Canadian journalist, touted the hypocrisy of most of the world on the question of American generosity. According to Bruce Garvey of the *Toronto Star*, "following news that the American Red Cross had run out of money as a result of aid efforts for then-recent natural disasters, Sinclair recorded what would become his most famous radio editorial, "The Americans." While paying tribute to American success, ingenuity, and generosity to people in need abroad, and making specific reference to the Marshall Plan, Sinclair decried that when America itself faced a crisis, it often seemed to face that crisis alone. At the time, Sinclair considered the piece to be nothing more than one of his usual items. But when *U.S. News & World Report* published a full transcript, the magazine was flooded with requests for copies."[13] Since then, it has been reprinted and replayed by many. The spirit of the address can be summed up in Sinclair's following assertion:

Our neighbors have faced it alone and I am one Canadian who is damned tired of hearing them kicked around. They will come out with their flag high. And when they do, they are entitled to thumb their noses at the lands that are gloating over their present troubles.[14]

AMERICAN CHARITY BEGINS AT HOME

America's is not a story of perfection. Rather, it is an epic drama about perfecting principles and values. This nation, born of the eloquence of philosophical and moral principle, was also accursed with slavery. There is no intention to recount that here save to say that the institution and all its trappings were anathema to everything our founding doctrines espoused. But this nation fought a Civil War, both physically and mentally, to put itself right. No doubt it takes a generous and charitable spirit to right public wrongs. And everywhere, from the abolitionist societies to the "improvement associations"—including the storied and prestigious NAACP (National Association for the Advancement of Colored People), together with more than a dozen black colleges—this society has done more than others to meet the substance of its founding principles.

It is perhaps this that led the French intellectual Alexis de Tocqueville to say 175 years ago: "The greatness of America lies not in being more enlightened than any other nation, but rather in her ability to repair her faults."[15] These "faults" were those imperfections with which this nation struggled from its beginning, and de Tocqueville's sentiments reflect the American commitment from the moment of our founding to become a more perfect union.

In the spirit of that commitment, American generosity at home is exhibited in the many associations established for the improvement of the lives of our fellow citizens. It can be seen in the history of charitable giving evidenced by the many parks, museums, libraries, and institutions—like the Lincoln, Reagan or Kennedy centers—aimed at keeping the cultural arts before the general public. This giving spirit has seen an unprecedented cultivation in our time with Warren Buffett and Bill Gates, in gratitude for the wealth the American system has fostered for them, committing to give away—and inspiring others to join them in pledging—90 percent of their wealth to charitable causes. Their decision was preceded by Ted Turner's announcement that he would give $1 billion to the United Nations for the development of mechanisms to secure nuclear materials.

These are obviously examples of American generosity exhibited on a huge scale by famous Americans. Yet there are also modest, more personal examples exhibited by everyday Americans.

This American attitude of generosity is often seen in the midst of a disaster, when citizens come forward to offer both their time and financial support without the prodding or appeal of government. In the aftermath of 9/11, we saw firefighters, nurses, and ordinary citizens travel to New York to assist those who were engaged in the recovery and cleanup process. In the aftermath of Hurricane Katrina that devastated New Orleans and many other parts of the Gulf Coast, citizens from states near and far and from all walks of life gave of their time, energy, and kindness, bringing food, supplies, and comfort to those who were in such great need.

Despite our faults and our shortcomings, we were a nation, society, and family within which the peculiar character of our civic values remained undoubted. From the Irish and Italian communities stretching along the eastern seaboard, to the Polish communities settling the Midwest, to the Scandinavian communities who immigrated to the north, to the Dutch settlements in the northwest, together with those who accepted the challenge to "Go West" and the Hispanics who dotted the country from Miami to San Diego—this symphony of cultures, while maintaining their individual character, melded together to become one nation.

When American actions depart from those aims and ideals at the core of our existence, it is also in America where that departure and the correction of a misguided course can gain a credible audience. It is in America where citizens are offered the most freedom to criticize leaders and protest against decisions that take us off course and where, in the form of its elections, it can remove those from power who have taken the country in the wrong direction.

Beneath the travails in our nation's history, there has always been something solid, that seemed as permanent in times of trial as it feels absent now: There was a unifying civic value, which even when unexpressed, bound this nation together. That value and its power to unify drove our sense of national greatness and generosity, based upon individual liberty, personal responsibility, and opportunity through limited government, exercised in prudence. These were exhibited in our national work ethic, in the protection of property born of that work, secured by the rule of law, and confirmed—often, if not mostly—around our dinner tables and injected each evening into our living rooms by the likes of Walter Cronkite and Harry Reasoner.

AFTER GREATNESS

It is important to understand the difference between nationalism and patriotism. Albert Einstein said, "Nationalism is the measles of mankind," referring to the conflicts in Europe in which each nation or group of ethnic people asserted their inherent right to be or become master of the fates of a host of other peoples. These are not the inclinations or prerogatives of the American people. In speaking of the greatness of this nation, Americans are not animated by a feverish nationalism. I am not saying, however, that America does not act in its national best interest: No nation as large as ours, with the conflicting array of demands on its resources, can always attain a balance of interest even between itself and its closest allies.

Yet there is no other nation that has shown itself a force for good in the way America has. This is not nationalism. Instead, it is patriotism, compelled by a flourishing and universal truth that all mankind knows—including Einstein himself, who moved to America to experience it—that we are born free, and government was instituted for the protection of that freedom. The bright light of that freedom is evidenced in America as in no other place. The happiness we have pursued has brought significant prosperity at home and generosity abroad, leading the venerable American foreign policy scholar Jeane Kirkpatrick to quip, "Americans need to face the truth about themselves, no matter how pleasant it is."

Now:
America *in* Decline

"Friends and neighbors complain that taxes are indeed very heavy," wrote Benjamin Franklin, "and if those laid on by the government were the only ones we had to pay, we might the more easily discharge them; but we have many others, and much more grievous to some of us. We are taxed twice as much by our idleness, three times as much by our pride, and four times as much by our folly." There is little doubt the lives of most Americans are being taxed in economic ways. But the real question is whether we are more taxed by our own shortcomings.

In the end, America's standing is not the responsibility of its government. America's standing rises and falls on Americans. This is why Theodore Roosevelt said, "The things that will destroy America are prosperity-at-any-price, peace-at-any-price, safety-first instead of duty-first, the love of soft living, and the get-rich-quick theory of life." It is time each of us looks in the mirror and reflects honestly on whether we are guilty of some—or all—of these indulgences. We must be honest about our reality before America can see authentic, lasting change.

4

THE PARADOX OF PROSPERITY

The danger to America is not in the direction of the failure to maintain its economic position, but in the direction of the failure to maintain its ideals.

—CALVIN COOLIDGE

As Americans, we live with a constant, unrelenting paradox: The more prosperous we become, the more susceptible we are to abandoning the very values, principles, and conduct that created the prosperity in the first place. Jack Welch is the legendary former CEO of General Electric who engineered twenty-one consecutive quarters of growth for his company. He always took the view that no matter how successful you are, at the very moment of that success, the wrong attitude can cause you to deviate from the principles and conduct that made you successful, and thus from that great success can come unforeseen failure.

There are those, of course, who say that America cannot fail, that the nation is eternal because—as shown in previous chapters—the nation has a history of greatness. But that greatness remains only if the nation's values are put into practice every day. We can look to the history of the Roman Empire for signs of our own decline and to help us judge the destructive impact of abandoning those principles that lead to greatness and prosperity. It also highlights the significance and urgency of returning our nation to its founding values and principles that we seem to have abandoned.

In *The History of the Decline and Fall of the Roman Empire*, the great English historian Edward Gibbon wrote:

> The decline of Rome was the natural and inevitable effect of immoderate greatness. Prosperity ripened the principle of decay; the causes of destruction multiplied with the extent of conquest; and as soon as time or accident had removed the artificial supports, the stupendous fabric yielded to the pressure of its own weight . . . The victorious legions . . . acquired the vices of strangers and mercenaries, . . . oppressed the freedom of the republic, and afterwards violated the majesty of the [emperor]. The emperors, anxious for their personal safety and the public peace, were reduced to the base expedient of corrupting the discipline, which rendered them . . . formidable to their sovereign and to the enemy.[16]

What happened in Rome, exactly?

A civilization of "immoderate greatness" allowed "prosperity to ripen the principle of decay," so that even continued success led only to diminishing returns, weakening the will of soldiers to undertake the sacrifices necessary to maintain the strength and safety of the nation. Hubris cultivated excesses and the defenders of the republic violated "the purple"—the imperial empire for which they were once prepared to die. Soon the rules that governed conduct fell away. The prudence that made each citizen a formidable representative of the nation dissolved. The bravest warriors took residence in foreign lands and forgot the nation's values. Then in hubris they misjudged their enemy, and the Roman Empire was struck from the face of history by weapons of their own making.

Psychologically, Rome was defeated as a result of the fall from its values, which in its population led to an attitude, a spirit, and a culture of entitlement. There was only the desire for status and notoriety and the material things that went with them, without the slightest intention of earning that status through the more noble exercise of personal responsibility and a commitment to the empire's values.

What trends are now visible in America that were invisible or simply ignored in ancient Rome?

- **Diminishing returns** arise when engaging in a process over and over again, at the same or higher costs, but with less and less beneficial results.
- **Hubris** is resisting the experience, criticism, and advice that is the path back to founding values.
- **Unintended consequences** are those outcomes that are unforeseeable and unexpected as a result of one assuming one knows intimately all the outcomes that will result from his decisions or actions.
- **Fatal conceit** is the result of becoming deluded by our own vain ambition to the point that even in the face of failure and great loss of blood, treasure, and reputation, we insist that our assumptions hold true and continue with the same course of conduct.

Any human institution—an economy, a branch of government, a school, a family—carries a natural risk of some or all of these trends. Great philosophers and scholars from Aristotle to Friedrich A. Hayek have tried to teach restraint in our perception of our ability to manage human systems, warning of these paradoxes that are sure to emerge. When we do not practice restraint, we become enslaved to a number of unfortunate outcomes:

1. We get carried away with our own success and forget the rules, conduct, and discipline that made us successful in the first place.
2. We do the same thing over and over, failing more and more often, yet expecting a different result.
3. We misread our own abilities and in the end do more harm than good.
4. We act with certainty, yet with limited knowledge—sometimes copying someone or something without really understanding it—and end up with a result radically different from what we expected because of what we didn't know.
5. We insist on a means or method of doing things that leads to contentious debate rather than substantive reform.
6. We equate authority and power with knowledge or wisdom, and we insist that others follow our lead, refusing to consider both the evidence and the possibility that our path may not be the right one.

DIMINISHING RETURNS

In all endeavors to establish a human institution—whether building and managing a family, a corporation, or a country—there is a law of diminishing returns, which is the tendency of a process to eventually produce less than it produced originally or less than was reasonably expected. Why do the benefits from our commitments and efforts tend to decline and dissipate? Because the individual, company, or nation becomes unreasonably confident in its successes and, over time, loses the discipline that fostered success in the first place.

But how does the law of diminishing returns apply to American prosperity and the decline of our values? Let's consider a hypothetical prosperous country. A generation of people believed in and applied the country's values and so created great wealth and prosperity. They wanted their children to have a better life, so parents gave their children the benefits which they, the parents alone, worked for. The children enjoyed the benefits but did not have to work for them. Consequently, the children never learned and understood the values on which the country was founded. They did not realize or understand how those values created opportunities that inspired their parents, or how their parents labored gratefully and sacrificed willingly, saved, and lived to sustain and protect the prosperity they came to enjoy. The children who were the very beneficiaries of the prosperity thus developed a diminished capacity to produce the wealth and sustain the economic standard of living their parents gave them.

It is upon this "tipping point" that America now hangs. Ironically, its next generation cannot "generate" the next stage of wealth or productive technologies or social progress that ensures and secures America's wealth, influence, and prestige, even though they have had every privilege a nation can afford to give its young people.

HUBRIS

The *Titanic* was not only an example of an engineering marvel; it also illustrates the human tendency to misread technological success as a triumph of mankind over nature. Given the great prosperity of America and our inflated perception of our capacity to control our fate and fortune, one must wonder whether future generations will say of us what we now say about those who held a near divine belief in the *Titanic*. Hubris almost always results in disaster and ruin.

Nothing that occurred the night the *Titanic* sank was inevitable. The passenger steamship sank because of the belief it was unsinkable. Because it was thought to be unsinkable, there were lifeboats for only 1,178 people, although the ship's capacity was 3,547 passengers. And so 1,517 people died not because the boat sank but because the builders did not provide for the possibility that it could sink. Because it was believed to be unsinkable, when the radio operators of the *Amerika*—another luxury ocean liner—called to tell the *Titanic* to beware of icebergs, the message was ignored. The misplaced attitude of invincibility is what caused so many lives to be lost, thereby undermining the very technological advancement it created.

There is no end to the episodes of over self-confidence to which we are exposed and in which we are complicit every day of our lives; we are blinded by mankind's tendency not to see clearly the circumstances of our human condition. We fail to understand that our continued success cannot come merely from past success; the greatness of America cannot be made greater by constantly bragging about what we have been. It cannot continue or survive once we have become disconnected from the values that created it, even if in that disconnected state we achieve some further success. We must value the ability to ask whether even our successes are true successes, or whether they are such marginal gains that we should discard them as evidence that we are on the right course.

Is America a great steamer carrying both the wealthiest and the poorest passengers that has forgotten its limits and is ignoring the warning signs of its own demise? Have we forgotten that no matter our power and influence in the world, we cannot overrun or outrun nature, and that we must and will pay a price for excess and indulgence?

Great nations, companies, and people can lose perspective and begin to think the rules do not apply to them. Worse, they begin to ignore the very discipline and processes that made them great. Proud and vain, they believe they no longer need discipline or process and are above any limitations, which nearly always, again, leads to catastrophe. This is the paradox of hubris.

UNINTENDED CONSEQUENCES

In human situations, some things we do for good end up doing more harm. *American Heritage* magazine published an article on bicycle helmets, which began to be mandatory in various states in the 1970s, observing: "By 2001, the CPSC reported, 69 percent of child cyclists and 43 percent of adults . . . wore helmets. Yet this apparent success has turned up a paradox . . . From 1991 to 2001 the surge in helmets was accompanied by a decline in ridership and an increase in cyclist accidents, resulting in 51 percent more head injuries per bicyclist."[17]

Similarly, in the November 12, 2009, edition of the *Wall Street Journal*, the paper reported on problems with NFL helmets. "'Some people have advocated for years to take the helmet off . . . ,' says Fred Mueller, a University of North Carolina professor who studies head injuries . . . The first hard-shell helmets . . . weren't designed to prevent concussions but to prevent players . . . from suffering catastrophic injuries . . . These helmets . . . also created a sense of invulnerability that encouraged players to collide more forcefully and more often." The use of a piece of equipment designed to reduce player injuries has, in fact, caused more injuries.

These examples from American pop culture illustrate the concept of unintended consequences, but let's look at a sociopolitical example to understand the true weight of this problem. When the U.S. government imposed quotas on imports of steel instead of cutting taxes on steel production, they thought they were protecting American steel companies and steelworkers from price-based competition. While the quotas do help steel companies, they also make it harder for U.S. automakers to acquire cheap steel. As a result, the automakers have to pay more for steel than their foreign competitors do, driving up their cost of goods and making them less competitive on price. Consequently, they sell fewer automobiles because the more expensive steel means a more expensive car. So a policy that protects one industry (steel) from foreign competition makes it harder for another industry (cars) to compete with imports.

What is pernicious about this paradox is how even when we do what we think is right, the paradox creeps up on us. If we are not willing to recommit to our foundational values, to see our actions—no matter how sincere—in a new light, tied to the power of our original principles, and if we are not committed to a constant review of our perspectives— what Jack Welch called "creative destruction"—then we invite upon ourselves a litany of tragedies.

FATAL CONCEIT

Fatal conceit is simply to insist on an endeavor based on knowledge you assume you have but actually do not and cannot have. Austrian Nobel Prize–winning economist Friedrich A. Hayek wrote *The Fatal Conceit: The Errors of Socialism* to highlight the psychology of "government control of the economy" promoted by Keynesian economists. John Maynard-Keynes, the distinguished and brilliant English political scientist and economist, had produced a set of theories that, in themselves, were not socialistic, but Hayek felt they would lead to socialism. To him it did not matter what good hearts Keynesians had, nor did it matter that they disliked socialism. They had a habit of intervening in a nation's economy, which though well intentioned, authored only disaster.

In specific economic terms, Hayek argued that an economy behaves the way it does not because of any attempts at controlling it, but because individuals within the economy make thousands of decisions every minute. No government official can imagine their number and magnitude, and cumulatively, those decisions influence the direction the economy heads. This is called "the market."

The fatal conceit, therefore, is the moment when individuals, organizations, or governments face a complex social problem, and instead of rekindling incentives based on the nation's underlying values and principles, they attempt to manage the multitudinous interactions of citizens toward a preferred, specific outcome because they feel certain they are right in their assumptions. They believe their actions can and will produce certain results when it is entirely possible those results occurred previously for completely different and disparate reasons. They come to believe in an almost "sacred" duty to "rescue" the country using ideas they alone possess and understand, assuming what will be good for everyone based on their own unsubstantiated confidence in their "remedy" and a flawed belief that "something must be done." They then believe they somehow know or can direct the outcome, which by necessity is influenced by an incalculable amount of distinct choices and actions outside their control.

To assume anything other than a return to foundational values is to base decisions and models on false assumptions. It is conceited, and for Hayek that conceit is often fatal.

It is the nature of our existence that we stumble into these paradoxes.

They cannot be avoided. Here is mankind, subject to both fate and fortune, but as a reading of Greek mythology reveals, the tragicomedy of our situation is that we are prone to misconceiving fortune as fate and fate as fortune. People think themselves knowledgeable, but they cannot see how, over time, they lose immediate insight into what brought them to their point of fate or fortune. At the very moment they think they know best, however, they must ask out of a sense of vigilance, what is the meaning, method, and process that produced their success and how shall it be sustained?

It is this eternal vigilance that lay at the heart of the American Experiment. It demands of us a constant commitment to the values that make America possible. If you imagine that this all seems exhausting, then reflect that this is why, in America, an individual has a right to all that for which he labors, and government was instituted to protect the results of that labor, rather than to produce the results for those prepared to labor and those who are not prepared in the same measure.

We may now see more clearly that in a nation built on gratitude, personal responsibility, and sacrifice—where individuals are free to pursue their own interests according to their own talents, and by their own choice undertake to make sacrifices in order to exploit those opportunities—we have what Hayek would call a "spontaneous order" that describes our pursuit of happiness. It is spontaneous because no one controls it. The values, principles, and liberty guaranteed by law mean that every second, every minute, every hour, and every day, billions of individual decisions are being made without the permission of some controlling power. Within this spontaneous order each citizen is free to engage in his own pursuit of happiness according to his opportunities, interests, and talents.

We are susceptible to thinking we understand what cannot be foreseen or understood by any human being. As noted in the introduction to this section, we are in the habit of claiming knowledge we not only do not have but also cannot have. Hayek wrote, "The peculiar character of the problem of a rational economic order is determined precisely by the fact that the knowledge of the circumstances of which we must make use never exists in concentrated or integrated form but solely as the dispersed bits of incomplete and frequently contradictory knowledge which all the separate individuals possess."[18]

Though this remark arose within a discussion about economics, Hayek wants to show more broadly how our notions of government-controlled development or growth cannot succeed. While it may seem like an obvious objective of government, it is not, because its foundational assumptions are wrong. Hayek reconfirms in this passage the wisdom of basing American economic growth on individual initiative and individual actions—based on small bits of information that may only be known to that individual—supported by a state that maintains the broadest possible environment of opportunity, so that as many individuals as possible can act to determine their own success.

The very arrogance of thinking we can balance the interests of the entire society by managing the pull and thrust of economic life means—like the captain and engineers of the *Titanic* thought—we have gone beyond what any human being can know.

THE POWER OF AMERICAN VALUES

Now that we are aware of the nature of paradoxes and how they affect our perception, judgment, and decisions, and their influence on the outcomes of thousands of actions undertaken by thousands of individuals free from government interference, how do we avoid these paradoxes and put our country on a right path? First, we must remember that the very prosperity we enjoy can produce behavior—in the midst of our enjoyment—that takes us away from the values that produced that success. We must also use our values just as Jack Welch used his company's service commitment (at the height of GE's success he would press his managers around the global to tell him of any delay in the delivery of any appliance to any customer) as a road map. Our values will lead us out of the Paradox of Prosperity, away from diminishing returns, and beyond our human hubris. They will limit unintended consequences and control our fatal conceits. To sustain our discipline, we must dedicate ourselves to an unflinching, eternal vigilance in the awareness, knowledge, and practice of our founding values and first principles, and their driving mechanisms of personal responsibility, gratitude, and sacrifice.

The power of our values is that the principles and driving mechanisms they inspire lead to prudence and restraint, reflection and judgment, and finally discernment. Every individual, from the richest to the poorest, possesses the ability to discern—based on a combination of logic, knowledge, and experience—when something is out of balance. Individual liberty gives us the freedom to both observe and address these imbalances.

Recall the Lincoln Proposition, which recognized in the American system a gratitude for the system itself, dignity of work, and protection of the results of that labor. This is what we must return to constantly, what we must attempt to renew over and over again, and what we must recommit to in every generation by an active gratitude to previous generations and by voluntarily undertaking to sacrifice to uphold these principles for future generations. These principles must be projected in every policy of government, beyond party, ideology, and political expediency.

A prosperous nation may, in a variety of ways, lose focus on those values that made it prosperous. In the next chapters, we will explore these phenomena with the aim of understanding how we begin to alter the responsibilities, size, and influence of government (the State), grown vast and increasingly powerful in a vain and misplaced attempt to recapture prosperity where it falters by its own designs. The difficulty is, as we become more comfortable with government's larger role, we begin to lose not merely our dedication to our core principles but also the psychology of individualism. As a result, we likewise lose the capacity to find our way back toward our values and principles.

5

THE ATTITUDE OF ENTITLEMENT AND THE CULTURE OF COMPLAINT

Most of us in the United States believe strongly in free enterprise; but sometimes we forget that freedom and duty always go hand in hand, and that if the free do not accept social responsibility they will not remain free.

—JOHN FOSTER DULLES

As the Paradox of Prosperity has taken hold of our now declining nation, we have gradually forsaken our founding values. Worse yet, we have corrupted these values, often interpreting them from the perspective of self-interest alone or even abandoning them for the comfort of government initiatives. What was once a productive and inspiring focus on individualism and personal responsibility has become an attitude of entitlement, now seemingly woven into the fabric of American society, and the once prevalent attitudes of gratitude and sacrifice have been replaced by a viral culture of complaint.

This attitude of entitlement is like a cancer eating away at the American body politic, a menace attacking us from all angles. It is evident in the behavior of individuals, both in private and in public life, and in the actions of institutions. The notion of entitlement now has policy implications at every level of government and across political parties. Self-reliance seems everywhere to be either dismissed or under attack. And we seem to have forgotten that limited government begins with personal responsibility.

No nation can be great, and none can long maintain its greatness, where its people are infested with an attitude of entitlement, where its adults have left their stations as guides to the young, and where its government is constituted by leaders who abandon the principles of individualism and personal responsibility for the sake of extending unearned entitlements according to their own fatal conceit. Guided by such conceit, they assume they are capable of and charged with determining what an individual should earn from his own efforts and what should be shared with others who have not earned it.

Whether the unrelenting, metastasizing attitude of entitlement is merely a personal attitude in our citizens or is the motivation for policies that drive government programs, unless immediate and deliberate steps are taken to excise and replace it with the enduring principles of gratitude, personal responsibility, and sacrifice, the consequences will be devastating. The very nature of entitlement and complaint dictates that eventually everyone loses.

THE INDIVIDUALIST VERSUS THE NARCISSIST

The word entitlement means different things in different disciplines. The primary definition is a set of benefits to which an individual is made entitled by law, by a process aimed at just distribution. In clinical psychology, an attitude of entitlement is an unrealistic, exaggerated, or rigidly held sense of preference for oneself that is dependent on others; it is a symptom and habit of a narcissistic personality. Both views of entitlement occur when, in the midst of prosperity, we forget that our standard of living is based on the principle of individualism. In forgetting, we come to expect a "just distribution" that is not based on individual choices, talents, or efforts; we become narcissistic, our behaviors characterized by vanity and conceit. We rank our desires above all else, including the very rights, values, and principles that have provided our way of life, and we expect distribution of benefits to be drawn from the results of the efforts of others.

What is tragic in this attitude is that a person driven by a sense of entitlement expects benefits in disproportion to what he deserves, based on his own work. He covets from others gratitude for what he produces, yet he has never shown gratitude for what he already possesses.

Such people see every response or reaction to themselves or their behavior as an attack. They have no care to inquire why another individual may feel a certain way about their behavior. Worse, they cannot even recognize or acknowledge when a response to their behavior is generous, instructive, or enlightening. This state of mind poisons all it touches. It trades in what makes it feel good or what confirms its fantasies rather than what is right. It seeks no knowledge and respects no knowledge; it treats knowledge as an inconvenience whenever that knowledge counteracts its self-obsession.

We are presently witnessing this phenomenon across our culture. Creeping narcissism often defines itself as self-love or is mislabeled as self-confidence. We hear people who have engaged in behavior that is injurious to others demand, "Don't judge me." We hear pundits say to people who have shown little regard for others, "Love yourself." We hear pop artists sing that loving oneself "is the greatest love of all."

As a Christian, I would have to say that the greatest love is the one I have for our Creator for his many blessings and mercies; believers in other religions would say the same. But even from the perspective of an individualist, the claim that self-love is the greatest of all is clearly false. In practical, societal terms, the first greatest love should be a love and appreciation for all who have sacrificed for us and for all that we have been granted as a result of that sacrifice. We are born in arrears, but ours is not a financial debt. We are the beneficiaries of priceless care and concern. Our first duty is to learn, acknowledge, and develop a profound understanding of and gratitude for that, and to make real that gratitude through a growing appreciation of sacrifices for our entire lives. It is then that we develop an appreciation for the responsibility of being good citizens, having developed a solid basis for individualism that has cooperative boundaries. And because of our ability to appreciate others, we understand and welcome the individuality of everyone.

The narcissist—the person who has an unearned sense of entitlement—cannot do this.

What matters here is for us to understand that telling people—and children in particular—to love some nebulous self outside of the attributes that constitute the self is the first stage of the everyday casual narcissism awash in America today. Should the person who is selfish, who lacks consideration of others, who refuses to work hard to achieve a prosperous life, who does not contribute to the success of the community, who does not provide opportunities for others, really love himself?

America is a nation founded on the notion that human beings possess inherent value, and they gain social, economic, and political value by demonstrating they can capitalize on that inherent value, which the nation was founded to protect. What we must learn to love about ourselves is not something nebulous, but rather our capacity to demonstrate gratitude, personal responsibility, and sacrifice—thus living the values and principles upon which this great nation was founded.

In a country based on individualism, there is no point in loving an individualism that says I do whatever I want, no matter the costs to others. In America, we recognize that the extent to which we are free to act as individuals is limited by the freedom of other individuals. What we come to love is our capacity to use that nexus to produce our best selves.

Moreover, as human beings, we should love ourselves as the Creator loves us and made us. It is a reflected love, and it demands something of us. It calls for prudence and fairness. It calls for honoring one's parents. It calls for avoiding covetousness (a key trait of narcissism), as we learn in the Old Testament book of Ruth, and it calls for developing an active discernment that enables us to honor ourselves through the rightness of our actions toward others. This takes courage, faith, intelligence, grace, gratitude, and a sense of rightness that one can defend and present to others with confidence.

How does this relate to individualism?

Contrary to the attitude and sense of entitlement, the love God has for us and the (reflected) love we are called upon to have for ourselves because of God's love are consistent with individualism. These same traits are the basis for the founding values of America—our inalienable rights of life, liberty, and the pursuit of happiness—and they are the essence of what is required of the individualist. In this light, the narcissist is the antithesis of the individualist and so cannot do what is necessary to maintain a nation built on individualism. A sense of entitlement, of whatever stripe, cannot be drawn from the Lincoln Proposition, under which a person expects only benefits earned through his own talents and efforts. The attitude of entitlement distorts the meaning and operation of individualism by misappropriating the language of individualism and ignoring and avoiding the responsibilities of an individualist.

The individual in America, because he enjoys protection from interference by any other individual and from government, is duty bound to imagine and cultivate a life for himself. He must seek out opportunities through productive work. He must, for himself and his family and those whose dependence he accepts, secure the best life he can. In these efforts, he is protected from government and can enjoy the freedom of letting loose his imagination and engaging in those activities that best suit him. He must cultivate his abilities. Because he needs to learn from other individuals, he must develop a gratitude and appreciation for what they can teach. He must treat their instruction—whether he agrees with it or not—with sensitivity and respect, since he is the beneficiary of the generosities that grease the wheels of life.

It is for this reason that the "huddled masses yearning to breathe free," as the inscription on the Statue of Liberty says, bear any burden to come to America. They sense they can "make it" here because they are prepared to be the sort of responsible individual described above. It is also for this reason that I think the immigrant today (and here I am speaking strictly of those who go through the necessary efforts to come to America legally) has a better chance of gaining success in America, because while we suffer the increase of narcissists, with their attitude and sense of entitlement, the immigrant values what America means, and arrives here without the slightest confusion. He intends to work harder, save more, glean and gather every bit of knowledge he can, be grateful and gracious for the opportunity and happy in his pursuit of happiness. This is the attitude that is essential to everything that is America.

It is to this individualism we must return in our rebuke of the still growing sense and attitude of entitlement.

THE THREE FACETS OF ENTITLEMENT

The best way to excise the attitude of entitlement and to restore gratitude, personal responsibility, and sacrifice is to understand and combat the three dominant and pervasive traits of entitlement:

- A something-for-nothing attitude
- An almost psychotic aversion to adversity
- A near absolute disregard and incapacity for taking responsibility

We must explore and identify the damaging effects of these traits to understand the danger they pose to the American Experiment and how best to defeat them.

1. A SOMETHING-FOR-NOTHING ATTITUDE

People seek, often, to excuse themselves from the effort required to create value, thinking all the while they are in a position to demand value: "I deserve it because I want it" not "I deserve it because I earned it."

In a recent episode of *Judge Judy*, a mother sued her adult son for recovery of a car loan. The facts revealed that the son had already defaulted on a previous loan from his mother for a truck. She wasn't going to be taken advantage of again and was determined that he should pay. Judge Judy questioned the young man, and the issue of the previous truck loan came to light. She asked him whether he felt any remorse for having let his mother down once again. He replied, "The truck was a piece of junk."

The son's attitude that the first loan was for a vehicle beneath his dignity, that he deserved a more suitable replacement vehicle, and that it wasn't his duty or responsibility to show gratitude for the sacrifice his mother had made to offer him the loans are prime illustrations of the sort of entitlement thinking and behavior we have cultivated across our country. His something-for-nothing attitude had clearly overcome any sense of gratitude he might or should have had. Gratitude would not have allowed him to default on a loan and then shamelessly ask for another, expecting his mother to show a generosity he clearly had not earned or appreciated. Gratitude would have forced upon him a keen awareness of his mother's sacrifice. And whether the truck was junk or she could afford it, he would have a need to recognize and acknowledge his mother's sacrifice and the fact that he was a beneficiary of value generated by somebody else.

This is a display of narcissism and a demonstration of how much genuine productive individualism is under threat in our country. The narcissist has no regard for sacrifice and so can never show or give sincere gratitude. He does not recognize the difference between what he earns and is entitled to and what unearned benefits he receives. The something-for-nothing attitude is a perfect descriptor of the psychological impulse that governs the narcissistic mind. Narcissists simply believe—often because they have been raised to believe—they are entitled to have what they want, when and how they want it, without having to sacrifice in any way to get it nor having to show gratitude toward those who may provide them with some assistance or benefit. And if they do not get what they want, or it is not precisely what they wanted or expected, they complain to a degree that is unnerving. This is true whether it is children in relation to their parents or citizens making demands of their government.

Alternatively, an individualist respects his own labor and efforts, but he first recognizes the sacrifices of others and is interested in the nature of and reasons for those sacrifices. He believes in earned benefits and in repaying with gratitude the sacrifices others make for his benefit. An individualist, in the Judge Judy example, would never have been in the position to ask for or demand the second loan because personal responsibility, grace, and gratitude would have demanded of him another set of actions.

To further make this point, take a look at the debt statistics of Americans as of March 2011.

Total Personal Debt	Approximately $17 trillion
Total Mortgage Debt	Approximately $14 trillion
Consumer Debt	Approximately $2 trillion
Credit Card Debt	Approximately $800 billion

Even if you left aside the mortgage debt, the other debts arise from everyday personal decisions. Only a people who labor under the perception that they are entitled to what they want—but cannot afford—would put themselves in such financial jeopardy. People who carry these astounding debts cannot exercise their rights freely as Americans. They become tethered to their debt, in the same way that America's national debt limits its freedom of action and influence in the world.

Exploitive, manipulative, and capriciously absurd, the something-for-nothing attitude is a fast-growing ill in our society. What is of greatest concern is its prevalence in our young people. Should we fail to curb it, over time we will witness the destruction of even this simple beauty of the human spirit, so essential to life: the voluntary sacrifice for the benefit of others. No one will continue to make those small accommodating sacrifices for others if they feel that such sacrifices—which should be everyday attributes of humanity—are not only unappreciated but also expected and demanded. Instead of recognizing that these little gifts, these offerings of value regardless of effort, grease the wheels of everyday life, the receiver takes the attitude that he is entitled to them. This, beyond even the impositions of dictators, is the worst, most egregious debasement of individualism and the most fundamental threat to a nation founded on opportunity.

The American system produces opportunity both in the chance to labor for oneself and from the generosity of individuals acting of their own volition for the sake of others. Narcissists destroy both forms of opportunity, as the exploits of Bernard Madoff and others like him—selfish predators who used the professional and personal opportunities provided them to advance themselves and ruin others—show only too clearly. While there are still many Americans who lead lives of individual responsibility and courtesy toward those who show them generosity, it is hard to avoid the sense that the country is being overrun by a more vulgar tendency—one that sees fellow Americans as a means to an end rather than a value in themselves.

2. AN ALMOST PSYCHOTIC AVERSION TO ADVERSITY

Some in our society cannot handle the slightest discomfort, difficulty, or adversity without resorting to a state of semihysteria, which they often misconstrue as stress. In their minds, it is insufferable to be in any situation that is adverse, so they commandeer every person and every resource available to them to remove what are really the normal challenges of life: providing for one's needs and the needs of family, pursuing opportunities, and generally taking personal responsibility for one's successes and failures.

We seem to have created, perhaps unwittingly and with the best of intentions, generations of people who progressively suffer from what I call an "adversity to adversity." Too many American citizens simply cannot accept or tolerate even modest inconveniences. As a result, they cannot handle the little problems of life that are far less difficult than the challenges faced by the vast majority of the world's population. This culture breeds habits that are narcissistic, self-indulgent, and self-destructive.

Unfortunately, while I believe that in America we all have the potential and opportunity for greatness and extraordinary successes in our lives, the adversity to adversity has conditioned recent generations for mediocrity. Rather than being driven to become their best selves, rather than attacking the hurdles (often rather small ones) that stand in the way of greatness, many have been conditioned to accept a lesser life and lesser opportunities. They prefer, instead, to complain and blame their lot in life on their upbringing, on their circumstances, or on someone else.

If they are not driven to overcome these obstacles for the betterment of their own self-interests, why should we expect them to accept adversity of any kind to restore America to greatness? We are creating generations of citizens who have no interest in or gratitude for the sacrifices—some indirect but tragic—that have made their daily comforts possible: from their parents, to the institutions that nurtured them, to our military, which protects and advances the benefits these citizens take for granted.

What is adversity? In the context of this discussion, it is not suffering in the sense of someone starving in Mumbai or Addis Ababa. In a prosperous society, it is traffic, credit issues, crowded trains, or simply missing the chance to get into an elective college course. It is a host of things that go against one's general preferences. When he was host on the TODAY Show, Bryant Gumbel would often get into a polite but feisty exchange with his colleagues who complained of a "hard time." He would say, "Come on, it's just the blues." What Gumbel was really saying was "grow up. Life is full of little setbacks and problems, and everyone has them. Why should yours become a subject for everyone else?"

This growing trait—an aversion to adversity—is becoming even more prevalent and noticeable in our young people. This is of particular concern because, as will be explained in later chapters, if this pervasive attitude is not checked and reversed through parenting and our education system, it will gain an intergenerational force that will extend the tendency, habit, and practice for decades to come. What we risk is the rise of a generation that has no concept of adversity at all. One that expects at every turn not only parents but the entire society to entertain its unreasonable demands for the sake of its convenience. Ironically, young people's adversity to adversity cultivates a redundancy: Their lack of fortitude, perspective, and resolve means that eventually there will be no quarter in which their complaints about life's normal challenges will be indulged or tolerated, because the very world their aversion creates is one in which each individual is only important to himself and imagines himself as the only sufferer of the "slings and arrows of outrageous fortunes."

Every college professor across the country witnesses this attitude at the start of each school year. Multitudes of students proffer a variety of nonsensical excuses for why they need special treatment or shouldn't be held to the same standards as the other students, ranging from why they cannot take notes in class to how they cannot concentrate with noise. While professors want to be sensitive to young people with genuine issues, the sheer tide of "special pleadings" is unsettling and reflects the general culture of entitlement and aversion to adversity.

Still more unfortunate is that children are supported in these habits by indulgent parents, who are creating expectations in their children that the world is not likely to accommodate later in life. The parents themselves do this in part because of their own aversion to adversity; they conclude that it is easier to indulge their children in all they desire than to demand intestinal fortitude in their sons and daughters. So, they take the easy way out.

This attitude of turning away from adversity of all kinds is characterized by an imprudence that is inconsistent with our founding values. True individualists meet adversity with prudent ingenuity, and every day in thousands of ways responsible people apply such ingenuity. The mother who is attending grad school figures a way to get the children off to grade school, and herself to class, with everyone in good spirits. The manager figures out how to deal with a downturn in business caused by construction on his street. People accept responsibility for their lives every day without their petty concerns becoming, as Gumbel said, a headline subject for everyone else.

If you were to watch a football team practice, particularly before the start of the season, you would see the coaches putting the players through arduous exercises and drills designed to prepare them for the rigors of the season ahead. The players understand that to compete and be excellent they must practice . . . and practice . . . and practice.

Here are just two of the many drills you might see in any given practice.

Drill one has the players line up in front of a piece of equipment called a sled, which has a flat, rectangular, solid steel base from which steel poles enclosed in padding protrude upward. The sled looks like a line of opposing players. The players get down in an attack-ready stance, and when the coach blows the whistle, slam into the pads with their shoulders, using all their strength and speed. The goal is to push the sled forward. Coaches often stand on the base of the sled to make it even heavier and harder to move. The players keep pushing until the whistle is blown again, at which time they drop to the ground, roll as fast as they can to the right or left, and pop up in front of the next pad. At the sound of the whistle, they attack that pad. And so the drill continues.

Drill two has the players line up and begin running in place as fast as they can when the coach blows the whistle. At the sound of the next whistle, the players leap off their feet, making their bodies parallel to the ground, and slam onto the ground. Then they pop right back up and keep running in place. Each time the coach blows the whistle each player leaps, slams on his face, and pops back up again.

The coaches and the players understand that in the game of football, players get hit constantly, knocked down regularly, and bruised frequently. Thus, to be successful at football, you have to be good at getting hit, getting knocked down, and getting back up and pushing forward again.

Now, imagine you are at the opening game of the season for your local high school football team where you or your children attended. You are wearing the school colors, and there's excitement in the air. Your team has prepared for this day for months—they learned every play, studied films of their opponent, and spent countless hours in the gym lifting weights. Unfortunately, the one thing the players on this particular team have never practiced or experienced is getting hit or getting knocked down. Your team receives the opening kickoff. The player begins to run up the field and suddenly, for the first time in his life, he gets tackled. You can hear him yell as he hits the ground. He lies there uninjured except for a small bruise on his hip. He doesn't get up. You are perplexed and yell, "Get up! Get up!" Still he just lies there. Then he reaches into the back pocket of his uniform and pulls out a cell phone and speed dials the coach. "Hey coach, I got knocked down—can you come pick me up?"

Of course, this part of the story is ridiculous, because athletes and their coaches understand and prepare for the reality of the game: that in football you get hit, you get knocked down, you get bruised, and then you get back up and keep pushing forward, *every time*. A person can't say, "I want to play football, but I don't want to deal with any of that getting hit or knocked down stuff." If you want to play football, you have to accept that these things are simply part of the game.

While I am a huge sports fan, and I think football makes for a great analogy, we can all agree that our lives, our children's lives, and their futures are more important than football (well, except perhaps in Texas, where high school football is like a religion). So, by analogy, how we perform in the game of life will depend greatly on how well prepared we are not only for the intellectual tasks but also for the challenges and adversities that we will surely face. As our lives (and our children's lives) go on, we don't face fewer adversities, we face more. Things don't get easier, they become more difficult. The challenges and adversities we face grow in number and complexity. We will get hit, we will get knocked down, and we will get bruised (metaphorically speaking).

1. I believe every citizen in America, and particularly our young people, must become an expert in handling the difficulties and adversities of life. We must become comfortable with being uncomfortable.
2. I believe that the challenges, difficulties, and adversities we face each day as individuals and as a nation serve as the training ground—the toolbox, if you will—for our future success. I am deeply troubled by our current culture's readiness to delegate and relegate the role of handling challenges, adversities, and inconveniences to others: parents, spouses, the government. By accepting and promoting this culture, we breed citizens who will lack the necessary tools to survive, compete, and excel in the coming years. Wouldn't we prefer that they be adequately prepared to get up, brush themselves off, and keep going?

3. A NEAR ABSOLUTE DISREGARD AND INCAPACITY FOR TAKING RESPONSIBILITY

Another trait that is central to our current and possible future decline as a nation is the growing tendency of outright avoidance of responsibility, which results in the incapacity to either behave responsibly or be accountable for our actions or the outcome in our lives.

It is hard to tell young people they must take responsibility for their actions when, in fact, there is so little responsibility shown by the nation's most important institutions, public and private. The recent financial crisis, which wiped $5 trillion from the wealth of Americans and nearly brought the world to its knees, seems to have dissolved into finger-pointing among agencies, political parties, and bankers, with no one taking responsibility.

The problems that led to the collapse of the mortgage industry were long in the making, and many in society were culpable. However, no one has taken responsibility.

Politicians, always seeking to use a crisis to their advantage, have created a new class of victim in this sad saga—the homeowner. But take another look at the numbers for personal debt that I noted. Despite their situation, men and women—driven by greed, vanity, and irresponsibility—took on debt for which they were not qualified. While many homeowners have acted prudently, all too many others borrowed as much as possible against the inflated value of their homes, using them like an ATM machine to finance a lifestyle that their day-to-day work and pay could not sustain.

Now many of those homeowners are deciding simply not to pay their mortgages. They are opting either to live in their houses and plead with the government for an intervention, or to abandon their properties with no intention of ever paying the mortgages they agreed to pay. This has become a widespread phenomenon, and it is fundamentally un-American. Yet it is happening at an alarming rate and without the slightest bit of remorse on the part of otherwise ordinary, law-abiding Americans.

Politicians from both parties, who cheered on both the homeowners who took out unaffordable mortgages and the banks that lent them money they knew the borrowers could not repay, continue to see themselves (remember Hayek's fatal conceit) as competent to fix the very problem their irresponsibility created. The banks and financial institutions, these so-called captains of American capitalism, that risked their balance sheets for untold profits, have demanded and received bailouts. And now the money of prudent Americans is going to cover private losses, which were suffered in the irresponsible pursuit of private profit.

Who has taken responsibility for this situation? Not the over-indebted homeowners. Not the complicit and enabling politicians. Not the greedy lenders. Nowhere in these systems of failures—and blatant disregard for the basic notions of personal and professional financial propriety on which this nation was built—has there been an acceptance of the slightest bit of responsibility by any of these groups or individuals. Large systematic events such as the mortgage meltdown carry profound but subtle effects that extend over a long period of time. In our effort to cultivate in young people an immediate spirit of responsibility, we will find it challenging to explain how and why they should take responsibility beyond private arrangements. Yet no society can survive without this sort of responsibility as part of the public trust. It will remain to be seen whether the negative impacts of these recent failures at all levels will undermine the crucial message so important to the American way of life.

The attitude of entitlement reflects a weakening and decline in individual responsibility, and threatens the very values and principles that built and held America strong for more than two centuries. A damaging result of entitlement in our culture is an infantile tendency to stand on all sides of any issue, not because of some deep and balanced understanding of the issue but because of a desperate fear of the responsibility one might accept by taking a stand. We see challenges to our nation's founding principles in our daily life, in our political system, in societal trends. The real question is: Do we have the courage to reverse this course?

FOSTERING ENTITLEMENT IN OUR YOUTH

Over the past twenty years, I have had the unique privilege of creating and operating educational leadership, career development, and study abroad programs for young people from across the United States and more than fifty countries. If you have children, you may very well be familiar with one or more of these programs—the Congressional Student Leadership Conference, the National Junior Leaders Conference, the National Student Leadership Conference, the Global Leadership Summit, LeadAmerica, and GirlsLead. These programs provide students with educational opportunities for growth, both personally and academically, and have put me and my staff in contact with hundreds of thousands of families across the globe, from every socioeconomic stratum, as well as tens of thousands of guidance counselors, teachers, and school administrators.

Over the years I have met many, many outstanding young people who conduct themselves in a way that should make their parents and communities very proud. Unfortunately, I have also seen among our nation's youth the constant growth and proliferation of the forces of entitlement and complaint I described above. In fact, based on my experience, I now believe that what I have witnessed among our young people is epidemic in its proportions. Still more unfortunate is that parents, perhaps unintentionally and with the best of intentions, have fostered these attitudes and culture.

THE RISE OF THE ATTITUDE OF ENTITLEMENT

The attitude of entitlement is in large part a result of generations of parents who have abandoned the teaching of limits, failing to instill in their children the duty to be gracious and grateful for all they have received.

The intergenerational transfer of values was lost after that generation Tom Brokaw called the Greatest Generation. They built an America that became the greatest economic, military, and technological force in history. The children of the Greatest Generation, the baby boomers, inherited a nation—though imperfect—full of opportunity, with a strong foundation upon which they could continue to build. In their youth, however, the boomers condemned America—sometimes for good reason. The protest culture of the 1960s was in part a response to a failure of the "eternal vigilance" that is critical to our march toward our values. However, through a total rejection of what they perceived as the status quo, they threw the baby out with the bath water. They lost sight of the fact that what they were actually fighting for was a closer adherence to our founding values and instead rejected patriotism and faith in country.

In their adulthood, they unleashed a consumerism that required of the nation the very type of aggressive economic and expansive foreign policies they had once vigorously opposed. They saved less than their parents had and assumed more debt than any other generation, while insisting on government with a proactive social agenda. As a result of a perceived prosperity, built mostly on their debt, and in the absence of the discipline created by sacrifice and gratitude, the boomers initiated and cultivated the pervasive attitude of entitlement that now infects our population and our social and political institutions.

In order to correct these misguided tendencies, which have put our nation in peril, we must develop a process for instilling in each future generation the values of gratitude, personal responsibility, and sacrifice that the Greatest Generation exhibited but, sadly, failed to demand of their children. This process of intergenerational transfer of values is not to be practiced merely between parent and child, but it must begin there.

REMOVING ADVERSITY

Today we see "helicopter parents" who hover closely over their children and come to their rescue when children encounter ordinary inconveniences or face some adversity—even of their own making—where their safety is not in question. These parents are willing to undermine any authority, exempt the child from any responsibility, or do whatever is necessary to remove any adversity rather than hold the child responsible for his or her own actions or teach the child a valuable, if slightly difficult, lesson.

In a meeting I had with a dean of one of the nation's finest universities, where we hosted programs, he confided to me that in the previous semester, he received numerous phone calls from parents who were literally screaming at him about things their children found unsatisfactory at the university—from complaints about cafeteria food and an uncomfortable dormitory bed to a demand that the dean obtain a written apology from a professor who, as the student told it, was "condescending" to the class.

It may have been true that the professor was condescending, but a young adult has to learn to deal with that, absorb it, and gain a certain confidence in encountering it. The better course for the parent would have been to coach the child to approach the professor respectfully, without overstepping boundaries; to engage the professor, maybe not exactly on the point of condescension; and through the engagement, to ask the professor the meaning behind his words. Through courteous discussion, the professor might explain his remarks and his perspective; he might even apologize. Children must learn how to win people over through mutually respectful discourse. That is the essence of democracy and the beginning of self-confidence.

Now, we want the best for our children of course, and we want to protect them from the difficulties, inconveniences, and adversities we experienced that limited us or prevented us from taking advantage of opportunities. We try our best to ensure they are spared the pains, trials, and tribulations life often brings. But it is precisely these inconveniences, adversities, and difficulties that are necessary to teach and reinforce the values that made us, and our parents, successful in the first place. The child can learn these values only through adversity; moreover, children must learn them if they are to match or exceed the parents' successes and to reach their own full potential.

This is not in any way a condemnation of parents' good intentions or their best wishes for their children. It is a reality check of the pressures on parents' time, requiring them to delegate to schools and the outside world most of the interactions and teaching moments that shape children's values and attitudes.

More troubling are the instances when a child has committed some offense, acted inexcusably or inappropriately in some way, and his parents come to the rescue, defending actions that are indefensible. Instead of seeking to teach the child an important lesson or appropriately reprimanding the child so that he learns a value, many parents react with an immediate, often hysterical, rush to the child's defense, becoming aggressive toward any who attempt to teach the lesson. This reinforces in the child a dangerous sense of entitlement, which usually turns out badly for the child and the parent. Worse, it turns out badly for our country as well, leading to a debilitating culture of complaint and the loss of our founding values.

TEACHABLE MOMENTS

In my youth leadership business, we had a tremendous responsibility for the safety and security of the thousands of high school and middle school students from across the country and the world who were placed in our care, residing together on college campuses. Consequently, we had a very clear and fairly strict student code of conduct. Students and parents signed the code so we could be sure they understood what was expected of participants. Unfortunately, we were occasionally faced with a student who chose to violate the code of conduct.

One such example is a sixteen-year-old girl who attended a conference in Washington, D.C. She was an excellent student and had been nominated by her school's administration. During an outing on Capitol Hill, she and several other students left the permitted area, found a bar that would serve them alcohol, and returned to the check-in area at the scheduled time smelling of alcohol. Initially, they all denied any wrongdoing, but soon everyone but this teenage girl admitted they had left the designated area and had consumed alcohol. Incredibly, she insisted that she had not been drinking, even though she smelled of alcohol and all of her fellow students acknowledged that she was with them, that she had in fact been drinking, and that she had actually been the first to enter the bar and to test whether the bartender would serve them.

Drinking was a serious infraction and regrettably, the students were dismissed from the program, and their parents were informed of the situation. A short time later we received a call from the father of the girl who refused to admit her involvement. Immediately and aggressively, he launched into a defense of his daughter, stating that "absolutely" she had done nothing wrong. He was told the details and evidence of the situation, thoughtfully and diplomatically.

The father's response was a telling insight into the daughter's sense of entitlement and refusal to accept responsibility: He said that he was an attorney and that if we dismissed his daughter he was going to sue us.

We dismissed the student, of course. But the lesson she ought to have learned was lost.

We cannot lose such teachable moments with our young people. When parents fail to recognize the importance of such moments, even good children who do not behave in such an egregious fashion begin to suffer from an adversity to adversity and a refusal to accept responsibility. Undermined by indulgent parenting, overwhelmed by peer pressure or by societal norms, propped up by education and social systems that indulge these behaviors and attitudes, our children never get the benefit of the guidance they deserve.

I fear for so many of our children. Yet I fear for parents too. I fear because there are many parents who do instill discipline and ensure their children take responsibility—no matter how embarrassing it is for them personally—recognizing the importance of teachable moments. I fear because they send their children into schools, into a world, in which all their teachings are met every day with oppositional forces. I fear because even good, well-adjusted, and well-behaved children can stumble in such a way that they—even if for a time—forget their discipline and return home with an attitude of feverish disrespect, ingratitude, and intemperance.

Recall the *Judge Judy* episode recounted earlier. What is unfortunately typical in this story is that the mother indulged the young man the first time, and probably many other times, which contributed to the young man's obvious sense of entitlement.

Every parent should ask himself or herself this question as a means of determining the character I am speaking of here: From all you know about your child(ren), do you believe others will tolerate the attitudes he/she/they currently exhibit? Would others accept or allow the excesses of an attitude of entitlement your child(ren) may display? Parents must ask these uncomfortable questions: What world am I cultivating through the allowances I give my children? How am I preparing my children for the real world, in which they are bound to meet abrupt resistance if they view other people as merely means to their narcissistic ends?

I fear for this country because so many of our parents are the cause—although often unknowingly—of an attitude of entitlement seen in our children.

The situation is not hopeless, however. But after guiding, teaching, and caring for so many children from around the country and the world, I have found that it is only eternal vigilance, and at times grace, that keeps both parents and children on a disciplined path.

A GLOBAL PERSPECTIVE

I have seen what children in other countries are doing without the resources at American children's disposal, and I worry about our children's ability to compete in the new global economy. That, in turn, will affect our nation's ability to compete in a complex new world that requires patience, respect for others, and gratitude for their efforts on our behalf. How will our children function in a world that demands both the capacity to be open to and respectful of others' points of view and the self-possession to deny oneself a perceived benefit on the basis of a greater obligation owed to others?

I wonder how aware our children are of their many privileges, particularly compared to children in other parts of the world. I have been pleased to see companies like Apple mandate that no child labor be used in the manufacturing of their products in foreign countries. This should be the rule, not the exception. But we know that child labor is the only means for survival for some families in poor countries. It is ironic that children in our country complain about what they do not have and believe they deserve, or complain about something insignificant that didn't go precisely the way they wanted it to, while wearing clothing made by children half their age. Those children labor without complaint and would never even think to speak to their parents or any adult the way American children often do. I ask myself, which child understands responsibility and will be better prepared for the challenges, adversities, and setbacks that life will certainly bring in the future? I fear it is not the American child.

I am not advocating that young children enter the workforce, not at all. I must tell you, however, that from the age of twelve, I worked every summer for my grandfather, who owned a parking lot and weekly rental apartments at the New Jersey shore. I would start at 7:00 a.m., parking cars and cleaning rooms, and sometimes did not finish until bedtime. I gained a certain work ethic and learned values that are difficult to learn any other way. We must develop a mechanism for instilling in our children the necessary values that will prepare them for entry into the world as responsible, productive adults with the right spirit, attitude, and ethic.

A Fly on the Wall

Children are the beneficiaries of privileges they cannot possibly have earned. As such, from a moral perspective their gratitude should not only be a cardinal virtue but also an everyday expression: in the respect they show to parents, the grace they show to other adults, and the desire they have to succeed and make something of their lives because they know so well that others have sacrificed more than they can measure for the privileges they enjoy.

We must demonstrate to young people how children in other places in the world, who have less than they have, work more than they work, and have far more responsibility than they have, nonetheless possess a sense of gratitude and a responsible and generous spirit.

Stories are often our best teaching tool. One story we used to teach this point to thousands of students goes like this:

Somewhere in Africa, a fourteen-year-old girl is arising from sleep. It's 5:30 a.m. Her bed is a sheet of cardboard on a dirt floor. She goes out into the field to draw what milk she can from a goat. She digs up a sprig of potato and mashes that into the milk. She first feeds her younger siblings, leaves a portion for her parents, eats a share herself, and then begins her four-mile walk to school.

The school has no walls, no windows, and no doors. There are no desks, no chalk, no fans or air-conditioners, no guidance counselors, and often, no teacher of any real quality.

Yet at no time does the teacher have to tell the girl how to behave. Not once does she have to be told to pay attention. In fact, she is grateful to be in school at all, and she feels privileged to be there. She feels honored. On her tender shoulders rests the hopes of her family and members of her community. She feels the need to be successful for them as well as for herself. She feels that to her core.

In the late afternoon, she makes her way home in the intense heat. Bandits who care nothing for the dignity of girls are everywhere. She walks home in this situation every day, often alone.

When she arrives home, her mother asks her to go fetch water. The well is a mile away. Yet the girl never sulks, pouts, whines, complains, yells, or speaks rudely to her mother. She obeys her mother, and in her respectful demeanor, she honors her mother.

The evening comes. Once more, the girl extracts from that field and the poor, exhausted goat a morsel of food, then she curls up on the dirt floor to sleep again.

This routine repeats itself for years on end.

If you were a fly on the wall in her life, would you be impressed? Would such a child with so little, who lacked in her entire life what you threw away today, leave you amazed? I believe that her sense of responsibility, her good behavior at school, and her respect for her parents and teachers would leave you awed and inspired.

But here is the question: If this girl were a fly on the wall in your life, would she be impressed? Would she think she had something to learn from you about responsibility, sacrifice, and gratitude? Would she regard your behavior toward your parents, who provide you with so many privileges and resources, as one of gratitude, not merely in words but also in the respect you show them—even when they deny you what you want? Would this young African teenager say she is as impressed with you as you obviously have been impressed with her?

As any parent knows and will agree, correcting the attitudes and habits of entitlement is difficult, for both parent and child. Make no mistake; we are taking from our children the most valuable opportunities and tools for them to learn, grow, and develop the character, understanding, and patience necessary to succeed in an ever more demanding, difficult, and global society. It is our children who will, for better or worse, be required to address the seemingly insurmountable challenges of the future. I am telling you in the most sober way I know that this attitude and sense of entitlement and the culture of complaint that it fosters, more than anything else, will be the seed of our nation's ruin if we do not recognize its destructive force and remove it from our social norms.

6

REDISTRIBUTION AND THE POLITICAL ENTITLEMENT APPARATUS

That some should be rich, shows that others may become rich, and hence is just encouragement to industry and enterprise.

—ABRAHAM LINCOLN

Another sense of entitlement has emerged recently in America, and it is based on a worldview of resources that lacks any regard for the individual or individuals who worked to secure them. This stems from a "social justice" ideology, the result of which is to foster and sustain a sense and culture of entitlement— often referred to as "redistribution of wealth." The politicians who believe in redistribution do not view their primary role as protecting the individual from an overweening government. Rather, they believe their job is to ensure an even or fair distribution of the income earned by some for the benefit of all.

It is hard for people who believe this to imagine that others find this method of governance an imposition on the enjoyment of their rights. It is hard for people who do not believe in this way of thinking to imagine that others cannot see these impositions for what they are.

RAWLS'S PRINCIPLES OF JUSTICE

The basis of a redistributive concept of entitlement (taxing one group to give benefits to another) is, ironically enough, an argument mostly about rights. The argument runs this way: It is only right that the least well-off should be made well-off, or at least well-off enough to survive in a civilized society. Although this argument has been around for some time, it was only hardened here in America four decades ago, principally through the work of Professor John Rawls of Harvard University in *A Theory of Justice* (1971). Rawls used the "social contract" theory elucidated by philosophers Hobbes, Locke, Rousseau, and Kant as the starting point for political society.

Understanding Rawls's argument is important because it shows how the institutional thinking about entitlement has become mainstream.

As the theory goes, before there was civilization, mankind was in a "state of nature," that is, a state of barbarism. This was a period without institutions or infrastructure: no congress, parliament, or courts, no universities, not even cities or towns. Human beings lived in a wild, open world, doing whatever they could to survive and taking whatever they wanted. In this world, some men were strong and others were weak. Stronger men abused weaker men, and groups of weak men abused solitary strong men. To protect themselves, individuals got together and agreed through a "social contract" to set up a government for the purpose of mediating issues. (Things did not really happen quite that neatly, of course.)

From this perspective, government came into being to regulate the activities among the people who chose them and set up the government— government by the people. But Rawls took a slightly different view of the social contract. According to him, when mankind decided to invent government, everyone was in an original position. From this position, having never created a form of government and having no reference point to guide them, they could not know what sort of world would emerge from their decisions, what their situations would be in the new world they were creating, or what possessions they would have or what their station in life would be. So mankind had to make decisions about the structure and order of their new world from behind a "veil of ignorance," meaning without knowing beforehand what one's status would be—rich or poor, smart or dumb, powerful or weak, etc.

In Rawls's words: "No one knows his place in society, his class position or social status, nor does anyone know his fortune in the distribution of natural assets and abilities, his intelligence, strength, and the like. I shall even assume that the parties do not know their conceptions of the good or their special psychological propensities. The principles of justice are chosen behind a veil of ignorance."[19]

The form and order of society you choose, says Rawls, will be influenced by the fact that you do not know what your life will be like. And since you do not know, you will likely choose that everyone should have a starting point that gives them the best chance to advance in the society. The things that make up the starting point—health care, education, minimum wages, Social Security—are the result of a principle of justice that says in a just society, everyone should have these basic entitlements. Rawls argues that you would likely accept this principle because "the principles of justice are chosen behind a veil of ignorance."

"They are the principles that rational and free persons concerned to further their own interests would accept in an initial position of equality as defining the fundamentals of the terms of their association."[20]

In the end, Rawls's theory of justice suggests that everyone has rights and is entitled to benefits. In the original social contract, however, particularly as argued by Locke and Rousseau, the government owned nothing and was not the decider of spoils. Government was invented only to regulate issues among those who invented it. Under Rawls's theory, the government must "maximize the minimum" for everyone, ensuring that everyone enters the new world with the basic benefits. For Rawls, government was essentially invented to provide entitlements so that the least well-off are entitled even to that which they have not earned, cannot earn, or do not wish to earn.

In advancement of his guarantee of spoils, Rawls doubts and discounts that which has made and makes America great: the inclination of individuals to give extensively of their wealth for the sake of others. As with the Good Samaritan, this combines the spirits of self-interest and brotherly love.

To be sure, some degree of vanity and some conceit are inherent in a civilization based on individualism. Part of the drive toward personal excellence in a competitive context is because the individuals are necessarily and sufficiently endowed with a healthy dose of self-confidence and self-regard that they even bother to act in their own self-interest. The difference is that such people are prepared to imagine, organize, work, and earn their benefits through competition. Others are opposed to any sort of competition and believe that by right, they ought to have some part of what others have earned. To this proposition I cannot subscribe; neither, I believe, would our Founding Fathers.

It is important to note that American society, largely because of self-interest, produces the most renowned acts of human generosity, as exhibited by the recent commitment of a group of billionaires to give away up to 90 percent of their wealth upon their demise. Through private charity and public support, America has for nearly all of its history provided for the "least of our brethren"—the sick, the widowed, the orphaned, and certainly the soldier who risked his life for the nation. That is certainly different from providing for every man and woman to have the basic components of life, whether they work for them or not, guaranteed by the public purse.

REDISTRIBUTION IN PRACTICE

Rawls and those who agree with him must be of the view that the founding values of America are interchangeable with new or different values. Their view must be that the founding values should evolve and move closer to their impression of what our times demand. I take a different view. I believe that the founding values are fixed and eternal: a government based on inalienable rights, based upon the individual, and established for the protection of the individual; a government opposed to redistribution and the sequestering of one person's, or a group of people's income—the fruits of one's labor—for the benefit of another group.

If you believe the individual and protecting the individual are the basis of American values and you reject the redistribution paradigm that Rawls argues for as inconsistent with those values, then there are certain modern policies and political trends to which you must logically object. These include, among others:

- The bailout of the banks in the recent financial crisis
- The bailout of the car companies and the transfer of ownership in the companies to its unions
- The imposition of our democracy abroad (which results in excessive military spending)
- The recent health care legislation

- The failure of government to reform Medicaid, Medicare, and Social Security by cost-reduction measures, which are monitored constantly to achieve market efficiencies
- The failure of politicians to make the reduction of taxes and the reduction of government spending two of the primary duties every day they are in office

There are those who will say that at the beginning of the financial crisis in 2008 it was necessary for the government to pump money into the banks and other companies to stabilize the situation. I cannot agree. Our founding values do not allow us to keep profits private while socializing losses. As my colleague Professor Gilbert Morris wrote before the elections in 2007: "It does not stand to reason that if the banks failed during the crisis that all would have been lost. Rather it seems so utterly reasonable that cash players such as Mr. Warren Buffett and prudent investors of his ilk—such as Wilbur Ross, and others—were more than capable of buying up and bundling the best banks, which would have brought the crisis to an end." This proposition not only exhibits faith in our system and a commitment to the fairness upon which our system rests, it does so in a time of crisis, which is the moment when a system is tested and justified. It is in the most difficult and trying of times that we are most vulnerable to the instinct to restrict rights or forsake our values. And it is precisely in these times of crisis that we must be vigilant and hold true to our values.

It also warrants mentioning, and it is fairly well agreed at this point, that our government played a significant role in creating the financial crisis in the first place. The attempt to impose social justice and level the playing field by redistributing benefits through housing, banking, and health care legislation and seemingly unending funding and support for government-sponsored agencies and programs led us further and further from our founding principles. Make no mistake, this much is clear: The abandonment of our values led to financial crisis. The continued abandonment of our founding values and principles is bound to make it worse.

Whatever one's view of these issues and questions, there is no doubt that the philosophy of redistribution and entitlements has emerged as the driving economic thinking in our country and the default ideological position in this crisis, and their application has left us facing a deepening financial abyss.

THE ECONOMIC CRISIS OF ENTITLEMENT

Our entitlement superstructures—developed to sustain and prolong the good life for all—are killing us.

Entitlements make up more than half of our budget, the majority of which is distributed as follows:

- Social Security: more than 23 percent
- Medicare: more than 12 percent
- Medicaid: 7 percent
- Other means-tested entitlements: approximately 6 percent
- Mandatory payments (pensions for government employees, etc.): approximately 7 percent

In Figure 6.1, you can see that between 2030 and 2040, mandatory government spending will exceed government revenues. Put simply, this means that the monies we have told people they are entitled to will grow faster than government's income until eventually we owe them more than we actually can collect.

This problem is not limited—by any means—to the federal government. Of the fifty states, forty-eight are dealing with budget gaps at the time of this writing.[21] More than thirty states are facing forward budget deficits that may be regarded as "severe," totaling almost $300 billion. In California and New York, the situation has become critical.

California is insolvent and has resorted to writing IOUs because it cannot make payments on many of its debts. A host of problems are contributing to its financial crisis. And California is unique in that its systems of exhaustive referendum mean that its citizens have as much of a direct hand in the state's fiscal demise as do its politicians. But state institutions seem to have had their own brand of failures.

Take pensions funds: California Public Employees Retirement System (CalPERS) is the largest pension fund in America and the third or fourth largest in the world. It is larger, in fact, than some European economies, with $260 billion in assets. CalPERS's financial base at the beginning of 2009 had fallen to $186 billion, losing more than 41 percent of its value. CalPERS responded to claims of its demise saying its losses were merely "on paper." For

Projection 1

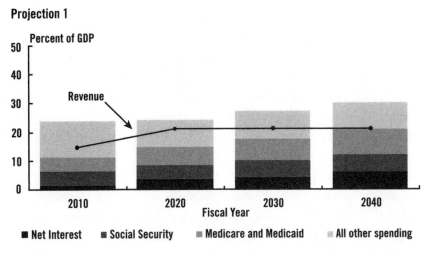

Source: GAO.

The assumptions of this projection 1 included the expiration of the Bush tax cuts (which were extended in December 2010 for at least two more years) and reduction in payments to doctors who treat Medicaid patients (those reductions were postponed in December 2010).

Projection 2

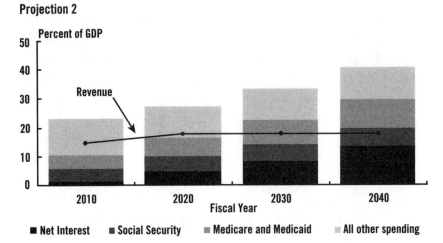

Source: GAO.

Figure 6.1—The Risks of Growing Entitlement Spending

CalPERS to regain its former position, one of two things must occur: Either the entire U.S. economy would have to head dramatically upward, which it currently is not, or CalPERS would have to concentrate its investment overseas in hopes of regaining its losses.

In New York, as a result of its well-entrenched entitlement apparatus, its governor says the state is facing a $2 billion deficit in this year's budget alone.[22] The state's comptroller said that state tax revenue was down as he encouraged—in fact, pleaded with—the governor and the legislature "to make some tough decisions now." Democratic Governor David Patterson did little to nothing to stem the tide. Yet ironically, in his 2010 State of the State address, he still admitted, "We saw what happened to a state that didn't know how to stop spending in California." And so, even in state governments, we find the lack of political and moral courage to reform entitlements through the exercise of the prudence upon which this nation was founded.

Whether it is the states or the federal government, this orgy of spending has collateral and corollary impacts on ordinary Americans in the private sector. They see Social Security declining and grow wary of the future. They see government employees earning, on average, 35 percent more than private sector employees. And they see these government employees, with little risk of losing their jobs, contributing nothing toward their retirement funds, yet retiring after twenty years of service with 80, 90, or even 100 percent pensions, paid with taxpayer money. And so resentment begins to build. Feelings of disgust and righteous anger build in taxpayers who have witnessed the disappearance of their own nest egg 401(k)s and now hold on to a diminishing hope that their Social Security will be there when they retire.

This is what our entitlement culture has wrought, and if left unchecked, it will render asunder all that our values, by which we gained our rights and privileges and from which we cultivated our prosperity, have given us.

THE POLITICAL CRISIS OF ENTITLEMENT

When we look at the policies of the last four presidents (two of whom were Republicans and two of whom were Democrats), one thing can truly be said to have been bipartisan: the abandonment of our nation's founding and guiding values and principles. Neither party, nor the majority of the politicians within them, seems to believe in the values and principles they took an oath to defend. Now, at the moment when America is most vulnerable, the principles that guided us seem again to have been abandoned by both sides.

Over the decades, politicians have ignored the critical nature of redistribution and entitlement—from policy, economic, and cultural perspectives—and pushed the issues off to future election cycles. Now the issues have metastasized, and the sense and attitude of entitlement that have grown up around them make it impossible to discuss them with any true honesty and rationality. In both technical and human terms, these issues become more and more difficult to deal with over time because of the nearly insurmountable cost and the politically sensitive, foreboding sacrifices that will be necessary to deal with their economic consequences, not to mention the partisan politics that surround them.

The political economy of reform is complicated by the fact that the budget automatically allocates funds to entitlement programs rather than requiring new congressional appropriations each year. As a result, outlays can grow well out of proportion to our capacity to fund them. Entitlements are on autopilot, and the autopilot is steering us into the ground.

In entitlement politics, however, it is far easier to play defense than offense. In 2005, when asked when the Democratic Party would present a plan to reform Social Security, House of Representatives Minority Leader Nancy Pelosi answered, "Never. Is never good enough for you?" Likewise, in last year's health care debate, Republicans prospered by opposing, not proposing.

"But while voters do not always reward those who make difficult choices, entitlement reform should be seen as its own reward, for without it, America will soon be crushed by either taxes or debt. The true compensation is a prosperous future consistent with our founding principles,"[23] wrote Andrew Biggs, resident scholar at the American Enterprise Institute for Public Policy Research.

What shall we do in this situation?

First, with respect to entitlements, no American—no one claiming to believe in the founding values and principles issuing from them—should accept anything called an entitlement, at anytime, from the government. Such things are fundamentally un-American. Given our values, however, we should view our Social Security another way: Given the degree to which citizens have paid into Social Security, it should not be viewed as an entitlement; rather, it was meant to be a deferred investment, held and grown by the government.

Government's excesses propelled it to "raid" Social Security, which was originally intended to be a secured fund. Unfortunately, successive governments have misappropriated these monies, and now the fund has become part of the architecture of yet another entitlement apparatus. Let this reading be the first day of a new attitude based on the old values. Let this be the death of entitlements in America. Part of the problem is how narrowly our politicians think of entitlements as a policy issue, and how little they include an American values perspective. But in deciding on policy, the first thing that ought to be considered is what a plan would look like that was based both on nonentitlement and on the protection of the individual's right to his earned resources.

Second, any policy tied to entitlements should reflect—as much as possible—free market principles. As Hayek has shown us, the best way to advance the protection of individuals and the best means to ensure that the best ideas emerge from a marketplace of ideas is for a policy to be the result of, and to be structured by, individual decisions, not by government mandate.

The moment the government controls our health care, our retirement, our futures, the individual becomes a mere expedient of the state. He is no longer an individual with unimpeachable value, possessing inalienable rights that the state was instituted to protect. He becomes subordinate. And, as in Franz Kafka's *The Trial*, he becomes a hopeless mouse in the suffocating maze of a mysterious and soulless bureaucracy. He is pulled and pushed through a series of doors by those who live on his ever-increasing taxes yet regard him as an inconvenience to the designs—however well intentioned—and ends they have selected as being best for him.

We must avoid the fatal conceit of thinking we can know how a policy will unfold in its actual operation. Therefore, in order to ensure that the result of any policy preserves the "look and feel" of America, we must begin with what is American. Therefore, every single government policy should begin with the protection of the individual: his choosing capacity and his freedom to labor according to his ambitions for the pursuit of his own happiness, assured of the protection of his earnings and the sanctity of his life. The formula and aim of every single policy should begin with these principles, and if an obligation must be imposed on the individual, it should be designed to make the smallest possible impact and impose the least limitation on his freedom. What we must resist at every turn is the automatic impression that provision of resources beyond the maintenance of the peace (which would include national security) is government's responsibility.

Usually this sort of commentary, opinion, or philosophy gets caught in the meat grinder of our political cynicism. We no longer listen to appreciate, learn, or understand. We listen now most often to react and defend. But it is my goal here to deal in what cannot be defended because it is the foundation upon which we stand that gives us the freedom to argue, agree, and disagree. I speak in the spirit of James Madison as he spoke in "Federalist No. 10" (in the *Federalist Papers*). There he warned of faction, that is to say, of being so divided that such division does injury of the country itself.

What could Madison mean?

Some people may take the view that in a nation based on individualism, such dangerous divisions are always a risk. I disagree, because that would be a false reading and a misunderstanding of Madison. In my view, as long as we stand upon our founding values, we can disagree, but that disagreement should never, in any case, amount to divisions that can undermine our nation since the nation means, fundamentally, we all share a belief in the same values and first principles.

Yet, Madison is also obviously right: When political parties in the grip of the various paradoxes we discussed each hold to unreasonable positions, the public discourse becomes intellectually dishonest. Hubris sets in, and the result is the rise of factions, each claiming an almost divine understanding of what is best for the nation. Factionalism certainly leads to a form of limited government since nothing is achieved by either party, whether in power or not. This brings us full circle, because what America needs is productive limited government that can only be achieved through values and first principles.

Limited government is a logically necessary proposition that is both consistent with the American principle of individualism and a central component of a more perfect union. There is no paradox there. Of course, we understand the need for a social safety net for those whom Christ called "the least of these": children who are not provided for, the indigent poor, the chronically ailing, and the aged. Because of these groups, to whom we have a proper obligation as a civilized society, all able individuals must do their part and pull their own weight to reduce the cost to the rest of society of providing benefits and assistance to those who truly need it.

7

DEBT, DEFICITS, AND GLOBAL WEAKNESS

He that is of the opinion money will do everything may well be suspected of doing everything for money.

—Benjamin Franklin

The Paradox of Prosperity presents us with a theory of how a prosperous nation may, without even noticing, slip into decline. The warning signs are everywhere, but hubris prevents us from acknowledging them. The astounding costs of our misjudgments are obvious, but our politics means each side trumpets our diminishing returns as progress and proof that America is growing and going in the right direction. We aim at stated policy objectives, and by means of unintended consequences, we end up far afield, yet our politicians spin this as policy success. And all of this hubris, these diminishing returns, and these unintended consequences are part of a dangerous psychology— a fatal conceit—a conceitedness so endemic that neither the crisis of the moment nor the lessons of history seem to drive it off of its dangerous path. Given our ability as a nation to grow and produce innovation even in the worst of times, some people are asking, "Is the nation actually in decline?" Do we not possess, even in our troubles, a high standard of living that is the envy of the world? Are there not in America, still, an abundance of opportunities awaiting those who are ready to pursue them? Is America not, in spite of our problems, still the most critical player on the world stage?

The answer to most of these questions is yes, but there is no guarantee the conditions they affirm will continue. With the ideology of redistribution rampant in the political arena and the entitlement apparatus that until recently no politician of any party was prepared to challenge in any tangible way, we can slip into economic ruin if we are not vigilant and prepared, now, to make difficult choices. Burgeoning debt, continued budget deficits, and a precarious position in the global economy that offers few options for pulling ourselves out of the morass are all signs of the quickening of our potential decline.

While many of us continue to enjoy the good life, we must examine the larger picture to get a true snapshot of our country's economic health and where our actions are leading us. Remember Hayek's point: The cumulative decisions of individuals dictate the direction of an economy and, by extension, the direction of the nation created and governed by and for those individuals.

EVIDENCE OF OUR DECLINING ECONOMIC HEALTH

There are many statistics we could explore as indicators of American economic health, but there isn't space in this book to explore them all. So let us begin with some key indicators that are often covered in the press, and then we will explore the variables that contribute to these statistics.

- Economic growth: In its report titled "World Economic Outlook: Recovery, Risk and Rebalancing" (October 2010), the International Monetary Fund (IMF) predicted that the U.S. GDP—a strong indicator of the overall growth of our economy—will grow 2.6 percent in 2010, compared to a global GDP growth of 4.8 percent and GDP growth in China of 10.5 percent. The forecast for 2011 is even worse, with U.S. growth predicted at 2.3 percent, global growth at 4.2 percent, and China's growth at 9.6 percent.

- Jobs: The IMF also predicted that the U.S. unemployment rate would be over 9 percent for all of 2010 and 2011. But that number reflects a creative method for calculating unemployment that produces a rate significantly lower than the "real" rate. It does not include several technical categories economists use to get a true unemployment picture. These include: "discouraged workers" (those who are unemployed but have stopped looking for work because they don't believe they will find it); "marginally attached workers" (those who would like to work and are able to but have not looked recently); and "part-time workers" (those who want to work full time but cannot find full-time jobs). When we include these categories, the real unemployment rate skyrockets to over 20 percent. Austan Goolsbee, President Obama's economic advisor, suggests that an inclusive calculation such as this may be more accurate than the government's official numbers.[24]

- Competitiveness: In its "Global Competitiveness Report 2010–2011," the World Economic Forum ranked the United States fourth overall. For most of the past decade, we were ranked as either first or second.

- Poverty: Of the thirty advanced nations tracked by the Organization for Economic Cooperation and Development (OECD), the United States has a poverty rate of about 17 percent, which is better than only Mexico's and Turkey's. In its report, the OECD wrote, "Social mobility [read: opportunity] is lower in the United States than in other countries like Denmark, Sweden and Australia. Children of poor parents are less likely to become rich than children of rich parents."[25]

- Prosperity: The United States is ranked as the tenth most prosperous nation according to the London-based Legatum Institute's 2010 Prosperity Index. The most prosperous are Norway, Denmark, Finland, Australia, and New Zealand. In 2007, the United States tied for the top ranking and has been dropping down the list ever since.[26]

If in looking at these rankings and numbers we feel that the numbers are arrived at through limited data, and the data analysis can swing many ways, what we all must do is to look at our current economic story, and get a grip on the factors that may contribute to these negative effects. Because more shocking than these effects are the hard numbers that reveal an increasingly precarious financial and global picture.

UNFATHOMABLE DEBT AND DEFICIT

We have all heard the numbers being casually tossed around—$100 billion, $700 billion, $1 trillion—when we discuss our nation's current economic condition. Numbers this large are beyond the imagination of most of us, and so when we hear them it is difficult to understand their true meaning and significance. We now talk about billions of dollars as if it's an insignificant sum. But it is not, and these stratospheric numbers paint a troubling picture of American financial prospects.

Here is our situation by the numbers as of December 2010, according to the United States Department of Labor, Bureau of Labor Statistics:

U.S. national debt (1.30.11)	$14.1 trillion
Budget deficit (2010)	$1.45 trillion
Interest paid on national debt in 2010	$414 billion
Social Security 75-Year unfunded liability projection[1]	$5.4 trillion
Medicare 75-Year unfunded liability projection:	$30.8 trillion
Total liability per citizen	$44,900 per person U.S. population, or $91,500 per member of the U.S. working population

1. The unfunded liability is the difference between the benefits that have been promised to current and future recipients and what will be collected in dedicated taxes and/or premiums in that time frame.

The mind has trouble grasping this level of debt. In democracies—even representative democracies—the people are expected to understand and have an account of their government's affairs in a practical manner, allowing them to play an important role as a check upon government excess. I wonder whether this role is even possible when the debts run at this level and the average American would have to have several PhDs to even begin to comprehend the maze of methodologies, calculations, and exceptions used to compile these numbers.

Yet the real picture of our economic situation is hardly known by those who say they know, and who should know. Because of the increasing partisan nature of our politics, we are more and more skeptical of economic reports depending on what institution formulated them and what they emphasize. Even the independent Congressional Budget Office (CBO)—which everyone agrees is nonpartisan—only scores legislation as it is presented to them. The CBO does not question the likelihood, probability, or rationale of assumptions made by legislators (politicians) when "scoring" the cost of legislation. It simply takes the assumptions given to them as true and scores the cost accordingly. Thus, reports are constantly being questioned by the other side, because any reports that show future projections are based on a host of assumptions that may or may not actually occur or be realistic. The deluge of reports from every political faction, each with its own agenda, is a classic example of our fatal conceits in action.

And a quick review of the economic data and how it is covered in the media or used by those in office leaves the unsettling feeling that such information may be manipulated for political purposes on all sides. For instance, even the number shown in the table for Medicare's unfunded liability is highly questionable. The day the trustees released their report, the actuarial team released a memo indicating the report was based on assumptions about legislation that were unlikely to play out and that the actual unfunded liability would likely be substantially higher than projected in the trustees' report. This means that those who compiled the report projected a scenario and built the report around it, as if their assumptions were correct. This is not how a nation in crisis assesses its prospects.

Regardless of how you want to interpret the numbers, these debts and how we are managing them, particularly the printing of our own money to buy our own debt, leaves us feeling that the country is broke. We sense it now hovering above us, and we feel it everywhere, on Main Street as much as (though unacknowledged) on Wall Street and in Washington. Research shows that we owe Asian countries so much money in U.S. dollars that they are beginning to develop an impression that we cannot and will not pay. This is a very understandable conclusion, because there isn't enough money anywhere to pay the debts we owe. An eighth grader should be able to figure this out. And because of our habit of printing additional dollars rather than making spending cuts to pay our bills, our creditors are also beginning to think the dollars we will use to pay them will be worthless.

Worse, the numbers do not do justice to what makes the most basic sense. Outside taxation, penalties, and fees for government services, the government has no means of directly generating the income to pay debts, pay down deficits, and offset liabilities. It is difficult to impart a clear sense that that money comes from us—and the government must collect it from "we the people." These debts are not the government's obligation, they are our obligation, and they will be paid with our hard-earned money in terms either forced upon us by foreign debt holders or imposed on us by our own government in the form of taxes and fees. The only other route is to cut spending and the cost of doing business to spur growth. That is our choice, quite simply, and that reality should be quite obvious and sobering.

The federal government itself recognizes the long-term negative effects of its inability to control national debt. In its June 2010 report on the long-term budget outlook, the CBO stated, "Large budget deficits would reduce national saving, leading to higher interest rates, more borrowing from abroad, and less domestic investment—which in turn would lower income growth in the United States. Growing debt would also reduce lawmakers' ability to respond to economic downturns and other challenges. Over time, higher debt would increase the probability of a fiscal crisis in which investors would lose confidence in the government's ability to manage its budget, and the government would be forced to pay much more to borrow money."[27] Added to that, large deficits mean "less domestic investment" and thus less growth, because less credit is available for business. That is because the government—at the same time we are in the midst of a "credit crunch"—is crowding out private sector demands for credit.

DEBT AND GDP: WHAT WE OWE VERSUS WHAT WE MAKE

According to current reports by the U.S. Department of Commerce's Bureau of Economic Analysis, our GDP is just over $14.7 trillion. Our debt is now also over $14 trillion (or better than $2 million a second), giving us a debt-to-GDP ratio of nearly 100 percent. In 2007, U.S. GDP was reported as $13.84 trillion according to the CIA *World Factbook*. In 2010, according to the World Bank, U.S. GDP was $14.2 trillion. However, during that three-year interval, our debt increased, our growth slowed, and our prices (and values) fell dramatically. This calls the numbers in those reports into question, and one suspects that our GDP is lower than reported and the debt-to-GDP ratio is actually more than 100 percent.

When we look at the historical measure of debt to GDP—our debt compared to what we make—an interesting picture emerges. At times in our history the debt was zero. From 1809 to 1814, the national debt was held to less than 7 percent of GDP. The average debt fell below 5 percent of GDP from 1826 to 1862. From 1901 to 1917, the national debt was less than 9 percent of GDP. See figure 7.1 for a complete historical picture of our debt-to-GDP ratio.

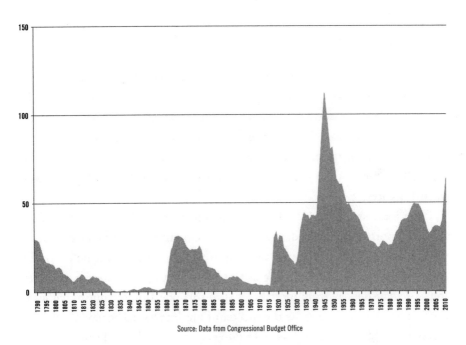

Source: Data from Congressional Budget Office

Figure 7.1—U.S. Federal Debt as Percent of GDP

It is clear from this data that the United States has been capable of managing its debt and, we might assume, could do so again in the future.

The data reveals that our debt-to-GDP ratio worsened as our entitlements increased and as we became entangled in long-term foreign conflicts that had little to do with U.S. security.

The United States maintained low debt to GDP during the First World War largely because we participated in the war for just nineteen months. We did not yet have entitlements at that time, and policy makers had been shrewd in their trade negotiations. American exports to Europe during the war rose from $1.4 billion to $4 billion by 1917. In fact, U.S. earnings in trade during the war offset nearly 18 percent of the $22 billion spent on the war itself.

This demonstrates a discipline we seem to have lost. First, it shows that in those periods of low debt to GDP, we have tended to "mind our own business." This was the true success of Abraham Lincoln's foreign policy. Second, as Colin Powell promulgated after the first Gulf War, to the extent that we enter any conflict, we must have an exit strategy going in. Third, we looked for trade benefits of the conflict to offset our costs.

EVER-EXPANDING INTEREST

More disturbing than the pace of our debt burden is that the interest accumulating on that debt may outpace our capacity to pay even the interest itself. In fiscal year 2010 alone, we paid $414 billion in interest payments on our debt. Interest payments have become the fourth largest single budgeted disbursement, following only defense, Social Security, and Medicare. According to the CBO, nearly half of the debt increases over the 2009 to 2019 period will be due to interest.

The interest on the U.S. debt has become as ominous as the actual debt itself and potentially more dangerous. It is recurring year after year, and when we borrow to pay it (which we must do when we have budget deficits), the total debt principle rises, causing us to pay interest on the interest and causing us to pay debt with more debt. It is to this question we must give some attention if we are to see how the specter of our interest to be paid on debt—creeping upward steadfastly—can lead to economic and social ruin.

What the chart above shows is a more compelling picture of the dangers we face. Interest on the U.S. debt is projected to be $530 billion by 2015 and to represent nearly 20 percent of revenues or government income by 2018. The fact is that the speed and frequency of interest rate increases can occur much faster.

How long will it be before our creditors not only refuse to buy more debt at the current terms but also demand higher interest rates because of the increased risk that the United States will not be able to pay back its debts? When they demand higher interest, it will compound the existing interest, increasing the percentage of interest relative to the total debt and percentage of revenues.

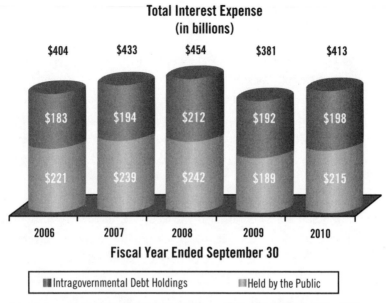

**Total Interest Expense
(in billions)**

| $404 | $433 | $454 | $381 | $413 |

| $183 | $194 | $212 | $192 | $198 |
| $221 | $239 | $242 | $189 | $215 |

| 2006 | 2007 | 2008 | 2009 | 2010 |

Fiscal Year Ended September 30

■ Intragovernmental Debt Holdings   ■ Held by the Public

Source: Government Accountability Office, Financial Audit: Bureau of Public Debt's Fiscal Years 2009 and 2010 Schedules of Federal Debt, November 2010.

Figure 7.2—Interest on the National Debt

On every scale, the news is bad. And the story of our era, it seems, is that we have managed to lose the country that was bequeathed to us.

TREASURY BOND SPREADS AND INTEREST RATES

As was said before, the danger is that the speed and frequency of the rate of increase in our bond spreads will be the most telling signs that our creditors have lost confidence in the U.S. capacity to meet its obligations. However, whether intended or not (you can decide that for yourself), the U.S. Treasury's policy of printing money and then cannibalistically buying up our nation's own bonds (i.e. the government prints money and then uses it to buy an IOU from itself) with our own new "invented money" means two things:

1. The interest spreads on U.S. bonds remain artificially stable, because we are among the creditors (buyers) on the demand side of the bonds.

2. If interest rates on the bonds shoot up anyway, it indicates actual creditor loss of faith in our financial credibility.

The observation here is as follows: First, we are buying up our own bonds, in part to insure the stability of the interest spread. In recent months, yields have returned to pre-crisis levels, leaving an impression of stability. It is reasonable to say that if we are buying our own debt, that "stability" is both questionable and not without consequence. Second, we must closely observe any widening of the spread on U.S. Treasuries. This would indicate growing unease by our creditors.

But it may also suggest another phenomenon that we all know: China and the United States are economically linked. We borrow from them; they sell to us. In the last four years, however, China has turned its attention to global economic expansion. And it is developing its domestic markets at home. It will take time, but eventually that domestic development will form a hedge against U.S. indebtedness. China will be less willing to prop up U.S. debt and the dollar, because developing its own domestic markets, and other resource-rich markets around the world, will cause it to become less dependent on the U.S. consumer.

DEBT HELD BY FOREIGN NATIONS

Aside from the sheer level of debt we have accumulated and continue to accumulate through our chronic spending, we face a serious threat to our global position and our economic security because of who holds our debt.

In the past, Americans held the largest share of U.S. debt. But as a consequence of our external borrowing, foreigners now hold nearly 50 percent of our debt, and they receive nearly 50 percent of the interest payments. That's almost $200 billion (and growing) we send to foreign countries every year; almost $200 billion that does not get reinvested in this country; almost $200 billion that is not subject to U.S. taxes and thus returns no revenue to the federal government. What does this mean for us? It means an increase in the leverage of U.S. creditors against the United States, with consequences for U.S. foreign policy.

The debt increases indicate a transfer of American authority and influence to foreign nations. As Figure 7.3 shows, China and Japan together hold almost 50 percent of the U.S. debt held outside of the United States.

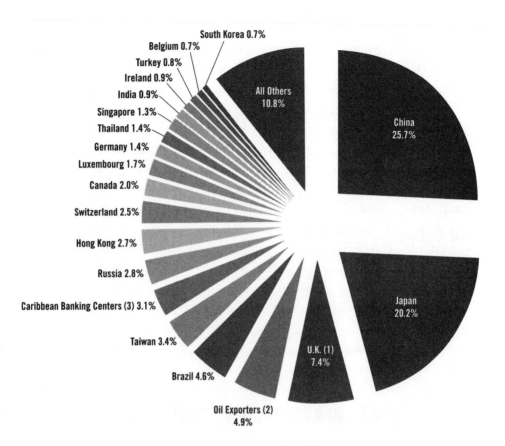

1. United Kingdom includes Channel Islands and Isle of Man.

2. Oil exporters include Ecuador, Venezuela, Indonesia, Bahrain, Iran, Iraq, Kuwait, Oman, Qatar, Saudi Arabia, the United Arab Emirates, Algeria, Gabon, Libya, and Nigeria.

3. Caribbean Banking Centers include Bahamas, Bermuda, Cayman Islands, Netherlands Antilles, Panama, and British Virgin Islands.

Source: Data as of October 2010, reported by Federal Reserve Board, Department of the Treasury

Figure 7.3—Major Foreign Holders of U.S. Treasury Securities

Clearly, creditors can demand higher rates of interest, which is a serious threat to our financial security. But they can also leverage their strength as creditors to pose dangers to U.S. security—by opposing U.S. initiatives and by using our own currency to essentially buy up the U.S. economy. I am not attempting to incite a fear of foreigners or to blame the Chinese or any other government holding U.S. debt. What I am saying is that the evidence is rather overwhelming that we are on the wrong path.

Old habits die hard. And government spending is the oldest of habits. No philosophy that puts the nation at risk to cover profligate spending should be acceptable to its people, who gained their freedom through self-reliance and maintained it through fiscal prudence. It is clear that both political parties have unwittingly engineered this situation. Without intending to disparage the Chinese, given our values of self-reliance, America is not supposed to find itself in a situation in which it must speculate about China's motives in the hope of its financial security. A nation founded upon individualism, diligence, and prudence should not find itself hoping that other nations will not act to exploit their leverage to undermine its ability to act independently.

It is reasonable to fear that we have not yet been visited with the litany of problems our debt will likely create. Key among these reasonable worries is the impact on our capacity to assert or project American power and influence abroad. This is also reflected in our lack of authority at home and the potentially destabilizing social issues arising from the political problems our debts will also likely create.

CONTINUED SPENDING BY GOVERNMENT

In 2010 the budget deficit was $1.3 trillion. In February of that year, the largest monthly budget deficit in U.S. history was recorded: $220.9 billion. Put simply, this means our government—both parties and all levels—does not live within its means and shows little capacity for prioritizing expenses, as every American family must do. This is obviously unsustainable and limits the capacity of our government to do all it should to maintain American prestige in the world.

SPENDING TO SAVE THE ECONOMY

We have already addressed how spending on entitlements is ballooning our debt and moving us further and further from our first principles and founding values. But we currently face another cause of government deficits that we must combat. In an economic or fiscal crisis, there is a tendency to think we can purchase our way out. However, this is not likely. Only spending that produces income to offset debts and will exceed the increase in the interest obligation can possibly work.

In May 2009 *The Economist* reported, "Having spent a fortune bailing out their banks, Western governments will have to pay a price . . . In the case of countries (like Britain and America) that have trade as well as budget deficits . . . higher taxes will be needed to meet the claims of foreign creditors. Given the political implications of such austerity, the temptation will be to default by stealth, by letting their currencies depreciate."[28]

These are the challenges to the state of our politics, which has dissolved into both sides demonizing each other and neither side being intellectually honest. Politicians—our whole political system—are focused on not losing power rather than addressing the hard questions facing our country.

Any individualist who believes in prudence, good economic housekeeping, and self-reliance cannot accept this debt buildup, given the values of the country he is supposed to represent. Is there anything we will deny ourselves for the sake of maintaining our discipline, which is the basis of our freedom?

What is stunning is how quickly an increasingly complex system of problems has emerged and overwhelmed the average citizen's capacity to absorb or explain what is happening. When the impacts of fiscal irresponsibility, financial mismanagement, and underenforcement of regulations, unleashed through sheer greed, cause the failure of what was once safe and secure, what are citizens supposed to do?

THE COST OF PROTECTING THE WORLD

We cannot discuss federal spending without addressing the largest federal outlay: defense spending. We spend more on defense (including the Department of Defense, the Bureau of Veterans Affairs, the Bureau of Homeland Security, and other defense-related items) than on any other area of the budget and than the defense spending of all the members of the European Union combined. Even if you consider just spending for the Department of Defense, the only single budget line item that is greater is Social Security. Consequently, hard on the heels of the economic pressures limiting America's global influence comes the question of the U.S. military. Given our economic problems, we are in no position to project American force overseas as we have done over the past ten years, much less expand that force.

According to a February 2010 article in the *Foreign Policy Digest* (FPD), "The United States has several hundred thousand U.S. troops or personnel stationed in countless countries abroad." Besides the 100,000–200,000 troops stationed in Afghanistan and Iraq, the article goes on to explain that we have nearly 85,000 troops in Europe, more than 70,000 troops stationed in the Asia-Pacific region, more than 10,000 troops in Africa, and a little more than 2,000 troops in foreign countries in the Western hemisphere.[29]

Given the geographic spacing and commitment of U.S. forces, many have argued that American military deployments have left its forces spread too thin. Likewise, given the economic situation in the United States, they argue that financing deployments at current levels is unsustainable from a resource point of view and unaffordable from a financial perspective. The arguments are valid, particularly when one considers the support presented in chapter 2: America spends hard-earned money to protect nations around the globe with little reward or acknowledgment. Every European household would have to pay higher taxes and so have less income if the American taxpayer were not funding their national security. We do this both because we are generous and because we believe in protecting the spread of liberty and human rights. But we must draw the line somewhere, and that line can be found where we are sacrificing our own economic security for the security of others.

In reporting on recent budgetary and spending plans, FPD stated, "Despite budgetary issues facing the United States that have derailed President Obama's legislative agenda and will lead to funding decreases for many domestic programs, homeland security, defense, Medicare, Medicaid and Social Security will not see any significant decline in funding." Fair enough, but that can only mean continued borrowing on the part of the government of the United States, increased debts, interest, budget deficits, and the potential of higher taxes and inflation, thereby further perpetuating and exacerbating an already dire financial situation.

OUR PRECARIOUS GLOBAL ECONOMIC POSITION

Clearly our economic situation is unappealing. There are several ways out of our economic problems, but principle among them is that America must become a net producer and exporter rather than an importer and consumer of the world's products. We represent just below 5 percent of the world's population, but we consume 50 percent of what the world produces. Investment banker Peter Schiff, in *Crash Proof 2.0* (Wiley, 2009), told the following story to explain the uncertainty about the future role of America in the global economy.

> Let's suppose six castaways are stranded on a desert island, five Asians and one American. Their problem is hunger. So they sit down and divide the labor as follows: One Asian will do the hunting, another will fish, the third will scrounge for vegetation, the fourth will cook dinner, and the fifth will gather firewood . . . The American is given the job of eating . . . He allows them just enough scraps from his table to sustain them for the following day's labor. (pp. 14–15)

In our current global economy, all the productive labor is being done by Asian and other countries and all America does is consume, with the crumbs going to those who are doing all the work. The Asian nations produce, America consumes; Asians lend, Americans borrow; Asians save, Americans spend; Asians sacrifice, Americans indulge. The Asians are doing the work. They are developing skills. The question becomes: How long before the Americans will have nothing to offer that can entice other countries to hold off cutting it out of the equation?

It is apparent we are becoming less and less competitive in the global economy, particularly in terms of trade. We can never match the wage levels of China, India, and Brazil. Our regard for human dignity and quality of life—while in certain instances has gone too far—means that we simply are not prepared, rightfully so, to produce our products in sweat shop conditions to make them competitive from a cost standpoint.

If we can't compete on price, can we compete on quality? We are still the world's technology leader. Yet a study conducted in 1998 showed that in northern Virginia, where the global Internet technology corridor is based, with more than 18,000 IT companies, fewer than 10 percent of the advanced technologists were American citizens. In fact, more than one hundred global languages are spoken in Fairfax County alone. The concern here is not the import of talent from other countries, but that the skill and expertise required to move America in a new direction, with the aim and for the sake of greater competitiveness, are not being developed and nurtured within our own country. This is what Thomas Friedman was attempting to show, in part, in his bestselling book *The World Is Flat*.

Even if we found the discipline to, say, commit ourselves and our national resources to a ten-year national education project to make America the absolute leader in future technologies, someone still has to buy those new technologies.

An observing eye must be kept on the health of other economies around the world, for their own lack of health will prove injurious to any attempt by the United States to lift itself out of the fiscal and economic morass by improving export trade, which together with spending cuts is the surest means we know to bring an economy into discipline.

Take Europe, for instance. It is the wealthiest continental enclave on the planet. But Europe is in the worst shape it has been in since the Second World War. Its growth rates hover around an anemic 1.6 to 1.9 percent. It has returned to its old habit of imposing unthinkably brutal tax hikes, without complementary cuts in indulgent benefits systems, even when faced with financial crisis. Europe, like many other areas of the world, benefits of course from military and national security welfare from the United States. Europe has not (and currently does not) have to pay the high costs of developing and maintaining a costly military apparatus necessary to ensure its national security and to defend itself from foreign invasion, since America, at its own expense, provides that very protection. Investment in Europe is collapsing and private consumption is declining. Because of the single currency in Europe, if the euro declines in value against the dollar, Europeans have little advantage in purchasing American goods, and we have less of an opportunity to export our manufactured goods to the eurozone.

So our options for finding friendly environments for improving our trade imbalances are diminishing as other developed nations are hitting slumps that may be far reaching, as can be seen now in Greece, Ireland, Spain, and Portugal.

How are we to gain faith in any solution that requires the support of the rest of the world? Europe is in the doldrums. Africa is constantly being reborn but is tied more and more to China. India is prospering but practicing isolationism. Russia is in a mad dash to God knows where. South America has a single bright spark in Brazil. And all of the once-and-future promise of Asia is bundled up in the emerging dominance of China. Russia, India, and Brazil do not need us. Africa can—as it has—survive without us, and even so, cannot afford to import from us at levels that give us an advantage. That leaves us in a ghoulish dance with China.

CHINA: ECONOMIC FRIEND OR FOE?

At the moment, China cannot maintain its current growth rates without American consumerism. Yet the more we import from China or move our manufacturing there (as the entire eastern seaboard furniture-making sector has done), the more we diminish our ability to maintain the very consumerism China needs. The more we buy Chinese, the stronger the Chinese are in strategic positioning around the globe, and our ability to wield influence, once commanded by our authority alone, is dramatically lessened.

The more China is able to export to us or buy American debt, the more China is able to import from nations other than us, thereby almost instantly restructuring global alliances in subtle ways.

Yet there is more than that at stake. In late 2009, in the *Business Insider Green Sheet*, Vince Matthews, director of the Colorado Geological Survey, highlighted some facts about China's control of manufacturing commodities that reveal how its global position could limit our growth potential long term. According to Matthews, "China is the #1, #2 or #3 producer in the world for 15 of the most important commodities; the #1 importer of copper, accounting for more than 40% of world demand; and both the #1 producer in the world of iron ore and the top importer."[30]

The *Green Sheet* continues: "China built 70,000 new supermarkets in 2005 alone." (For a little perspective on that number, the 2002 census counted about 150,000 total "food and beverage stores" in the United States.) And China's demand for minerals and other commodities has driven up prices: Copper was up 307 percent, scrap iron was up 559 percent, and molybdenum was up 997 percent.

China is moving aggressively in the world to garner control over the natural resources it needs. *Fast Company* produced an account of the urgency of this issue in its June 2008 six-part special report, "China Storms Africa":

> While America is preoccupied with the war in Iraq (cost: half a trillion dollars and counting), and while think-tank economists continue to spit out

papers debating whether vital resources are running out at all, China's leadership isn't taking any chances. In just a few years, the People's Republic of China (PRC) has become the most aggressive investor-nation in Africa. This commercial invasion is without question the most important development in the sub-Sahara since the end of the Cold War—an epic, almost primal propulsion that is redrawing the global economic map. One former U.S. assistant secretary of state has called it a "tsunami." Some are even calling the region "ChinAfrica." There are already more Chinese living in Nigeria than there were Britons during the height of the empire.

From state-owned and state-linked corporations to small entrepreneurs, the Chinese are cutting a swath across the continent. As many as 1 million Chinese citizens are circulating here. Each megaproject announced by China's government creates collateral economies and population monuments, like the ripples of a stone skimmed across a lake.

The special report continued, painting a picture of China's prowess in another article.

Beijing declared 2006 the "Year of Africa," and China's leaders have made one Bono-like tour after another. No other major power has shown the same interest or muscle, or the sheer ability to cozy up to African leaders. And unlike America's faltering effort in Iraq, the Chinese ain't spreading democracy, folks. They're there to get what they need to feed the machine. The phenomenon even has a name on the ground in the sub-Sahara: the Great Chinese Takeout . . . [31]

Says a leading Western oil expert who has been working in Equatorial Guinea (E.G.) for more than a decade,

American companies here don't want people to know it, but they are shitting about China. China is systematically challenging the American oil giants here—locking in exploration or supply contracts, winning rights to new oil fields, doing massive infrastructure development, even stepping up military supplies . . . America remains E.G.'s dominant foreign investor by far, with $7 billion in cumulative direct investments over the past decade, and with ExxonMobil, Amerada Hess, and Marathon Oil leading the way. But if recent statistics are reliable, China has surpassed the United States as E.G.'s biggest trading partner, purchasing more than $2.5 billion of its oil a year.[32]

We have a limited number of strategic resources—copper, soft gold (for super computers), industrial diamonds (for lasers), and so on. If the United States does not have future suppliers for these commodities relative to its demand for them and relative to its power in the world, America could find that the resources required to maintain its commercial, technological, and even its military edge are either held or encumbered by its largest creditor, China. A very untenable situation for America.

Yet China is in a precarious situation too. The United States cannot continue to spend and borrow as it has. However, the Chinese cannot afford for the United States not to spend and borrow. For instance, if the Chinese were to allow their currency to appreciate significantly against the dollar, that would ease some of the debt and could ease some of the unemployment burden the United States faces because, at least in theory, Chinese labor costs would increase, thus removing some of the incentive to move jobs to China. U.S. companies manufacturing in China cannot wish for it to do anything that increases the cost of labor, putting them at a financial disadvantage. Yet that is precisely the help the United States may need to narrow the disadvantage with China and position U.S. manufacturing competitively in the global arena.

Is there a path for America to correct its economic picture by exporting to China? The answer appears to be no. China is facing its own economic crisis. To replace falling American consumer spending, its banks began to lend, and there was a massive stimulus package in 2009. Now the Chinese are fighting inflation and bad loans and will be doing so over the next five years.

Here, then, is the conundrum: China needs the United States to consume because it ensures the movement of Chinese exports. China buys U.S. debt both to loan us money and to slow the decline of the U.S. dollar. If demand falls in this country and Americans cannot consume, China cannot export in the volumes to which it has become accustomed and for which it has built a trade and shipping infrastructure. A catastrophic fall in demand in the United States will mean severe price deflation for Chinese products, which will be in oversupply with few buyers. But it will also mean more expensive products here at home because our production moved to China due to the uncompetitive costs of production in this country as result of overregulation, selective regulation, and the high cost of labor, together with the legacy cost of labor, which our competitors (like China) do not have.

The situation we have created here in America will not go away anytime soon, and options for improving our global positioning are in shorter supply than ever before. Our only hope for improving our financial strength and using that strength to gain a more stable global footing is to focus on our own fiscal prudence.

A RETURN TO FISCAL PRUDENCE

Our nation has been the pillar of strength in the world, but it now stands at a crossroads. We must decide what we are and what type of America we want to be. Then we must work to ensure that we become the America we imagine, subject to the values upon which we were founded. The debt story outlined in the "Debt and GDP" section earlier in this chapter shows that we can be fiscally prudent and we can discipline ourselves by prioritizing our options for investment in growth and providing support for social programs that help people in actual need. Our debts, deficits, trade imbalances, and unfunded liabilities are of our own making. Yet America cannot export its way out of its crisis; the consequences of this crisis are a weakening economic prowess and a weakening of American influence in the world. We seem to have indulged ourselves and at the same time forgotten our founding values, in which individualism, personal responsibility, and prudence were cardinal tenets.

In spite of these obstacles, America can survive and thrive. However, it must discover a new competitive nexus so that we can work our way out of debt and begin to cultivate a leaner, more efficient government and a more competitive economy. To do that, we must first return to our first principles and founding values.

8

THE BROAD EFFECTS
OF THE DECLINE OF EDUCATION

The direction in which education starts a man will determine his future in life.

—Plato

American education is in crisis.

In addition to our political and economic problems, and in some cases because of them, we face other equally overwhelming domestic issues that indicate further declines in American prestige, standing, and competitiveness. The most important of these is our declining education system: record drop-out rates, falling test scores, more and more money being spent on schools that are failing. We are not preparing our youth to join a competitive global workforce or to contribute to the growth of our economy.

There is an ominous link between our economic plight and our declining educational performance as a country. Our failure to get our debts and deficits under control means we have fewer resources to address the problem of declining educational performance, which has the potential to drive our economic performance into further decline. And as we have fewer resources to devote to making America competitive in the global market, faith in our system will continue to fall. Our declining education performance impacts not only our nation's economic position, but also our national resources. It contributes to the creation and reinforcement of a culture of entitlement, because those without a proper education are less and less able to function in a sophisticated society as responsible individuals in the spirit of the Lincoln Proposition.

And eventually, when—as Plato feared—there are more "unenlightened" citizens than "enlightened" ones, the former will extract resources from the latter either by force or through a political process demographically weighted in their favor because of the sheer increase in numbers of those who cannot or will not fend for themselves. And a clear-eyed look at our "economic-entitlement complex" suggests that this process—taking from those who work to have and giving to those who insist they deserve with or without work—is already under way. The statistics identify complex sociological effects, such as the impact on prison populations, which extend the cost of the dropout rate to the rest of society. What cannot be calculated is the impact on the loss of "well-being" in the society, particularly as it relates to violent crimes committed by those high school dropouts who are then imprisoned.

THE HIGH COST OF DROPOUTS

In a 2008 article in the *Wall Street Journal* titled "The High School Dropout's Economic Ripple Effect," the paper presented some disturbing statistics. According to the president and CEO of America's Promise Alliance, a youth advocacy organization, "there are about 77 million people who are hoping to retire—circumstances permitting—and are depending on workers to 'fuel our economy and future growth, and the next generation of workers is not prepared for the 21st-century global economy.' . . . Each year dropouts represent $320 billion in lost lifetime earning potential."[33]

And as we have fewer and fewer resources to devote to making America competitive in the global market, faith in our system—should these trends continue—will not be sustainable.

According to the American Youth Policy Forum:

- A student drops out of school every nine seconds in America.
- Three-quarters of state prison inmates and 59 percent of federal inmates are high school dropouts.

- Slightly less than 46 percent of the nation's young high school drop-outs were employed on average during 2008.
- By some estimates, "the cost to the public of [dropouts'] crime and welfare benefits is estimated to total $24 billion annually."[34]

High school dropouts on the whole are most often a "net loss" to society. It is true that many high school dropouts turn their lives around. But for the most part, high school dropouts contribute less to society than their potential contribution, less than the relative cost of nurturing that potential up to the time they drop out, and less than the cost of the violence, crime, hostility, and financial demands (through entitlement programs) they often inflict on society.

Of course, it is almost impossible to completely capture the true cost of our ever-growing dropout population, but the economic loss we face is very real. The question to address is this: How can we expect to control entitlement spending and gain a global economic competitive advantage when nearly one-third of our nation's youth drop out of school and then go on the dole, resort to crime to finance their lifestyles, or are unable to make enough money to avoid resorting to welfare to support their families?

An entitlement culture finds itself in a vicious cycle of diminishing returns: Low standards result in poor schools where poor performance is the norm, which results in adults with lower standards. A danger of this cycle is that citizens can awake to discover that the public or political discourse and judgment necessary for an advanced society is not only unlikely but also, in certain respects, impossible. Thus the costs grow beyond the most obvious economic impacts to affect the very hope for and faith in the future of the society itself. Many scholars worried about this possibility, and some— John Stuart Mill, the nineteenth-century British philosopher was one such visionary—saw it as an eventuality more than 120 years ago.

Mill feared the consequences of the "tyranny of the majority," where the majority imposed itself on individuals, and the individual, because of the system of democracy, had little means to respond in defense of himself and his liberty. Although Mill wrote in a dense and difficult style, it pays to read his own words, which touch so completely on all that I have been attempting to say.

The "people" who exercise the power are not always the same people with those over whom it is exercised; and the "self-government" spoken of is not the government of each by himself, but of each by all the rest. The will of the people, moreover, practically means the will of the most numerous or the most active part of the people; the majority, or those who succeed in making themselves accepted as the majority; the people, consequently may desire to oppress a part of their number; and precautions are as much needed against this as against any other abuse of power. The limitation, therefore, of the power of government over individuals loses none of its importance when the holders of power are regularly accountable to the community, that is, to the strongest party therein. This view of things, recommending itself equally to the intelligence of thinkers and to the inclination of those important classes in European society to whose real or supposed interests democracy is adverse, has had no difficulty in establishing itself; and in political speculations "the tyranny of the majority" is now generally included among the evils against which society requires to be on its guard.

Like other tyrannies, the tyranny of the majority was at first, and is still vulgarly, held in dread, chiefly as operating through the acts of the public authorities. But reflecting persons perceived that when society is itself the tyrant—society collectively over the separate individuals who compose it— its means of tyrannizing are not restricted to the acts which it may do by the hands of its political functionaries. Society can and does execute its own mandates: and if it issues wrong mandates instead of right, or any mandates at all in things with which it ought not to meddle, it practices a social tyranny more formidable than many kinds of political oppression, since, though not usually upheld by such extreme penalties, it leaves fewer means of escape, penetrating much more deeply into the details of life, and enslaving the soul itself.[35]

Mill thought this "majority" emerged over time from the "uneducated masses," to use nineteenth-century language. He argued that eventually they become the majority in society and soon begin to demand the "spoils of society" without regard for the toil of those whose labor cultivated it.

Is this possible in America? Could it be that these dropouts, in their overwhelming numbers, do not reflect the nation's first principles or the Lincoln Proposition, and that they more readily believe in something completely different from the foundational values that made this country great?

The United States has 16.5 million students[36] and a high school dropout rate of 8 percent as of 2008 (though it declined from 14 percent in 1980).[37] That equates to about 1.2 million students who drop out each year, or more than 10 million people over ten years. These individuals will have little real capacity—speaking generally—to contribute to their own advancement and so to the advancement of society. Reflect on a voter roll impacted by these numbers over twenty-five or thirty-five years, and an awful specter of impending catastrophe begins to loom. Will these individuals vote in a way that will ensure the long-term growth and success of our society if, as individuals, they are barely prepared to contribute to that growth or success?

But that is not the most awful aspect of the potential tyranny of an unschooled majority. The more awful aspect is that the student dropout has a "natural multiplier" effect, in that it is likely that these dropouts will have children and that their children will repeat the same cycle of lost potential that preceded them. In this way, those who lay claim on society's resources without contribution may outnumber contributors to society. They may reflect—for an array of sociological reasons, some justified, others unjustified—a deep hostility to the idea and ideal of "upward mobility" that is at the heart of a nation built on individualism and the cultivation and application of human capital.

The purpose here is not to demonize this troubling sociological group. The aim is to warn that if we do not address the issues that lead to dropouts and the culture to which they contribute, the likely ability to address them diminishes every day, since the political apparatus that gives the high school (and often social) dropout an equal footing with those who contribute will not be changed by the uneducated masses.[38]

What an enormous disservice we are doing to our youth and our country by allowing entitlement programs to reward teens for failure, giving them a reason to give up when the going gets hard, and failing to demand that they contribute to our economy and society in a productive and positive way.

OUR INTERNATIONAL EDUCATION STANDING

If the dropout rate were our only problem, it would be a serious but containable one. But we face an even more complex problem: Too many of the students who do graduate are insufficiently prepared to provide the United States with a well-educated, trainable workforce. This is a major hindrance to our ability to compete in Thomas Friedman's flattening world.

In 2006, the Organization for Economic Cooperation and Development's (OECD) Programme for International Student Assessment (PISA) completed its third study of international math, science, and reading.

- American fifteen-year-olds scored below the average for advanced nations on math and science literacy, ranking twenty-fourth in math and twenty-second in science out of fifty-six nations participating.[39]
- About one-quarter of students performed below the baseline level of proficiency that would prepare them for using math and science concepts in their daily lives.
- In 2003, the United States ranked sixteenth of twenty-nine OECD countries in reading literacy (the 2006 numbers were invalidated due to an error in the test) and ranked twenty-fifth of twenty-nine OECD countries in problem solving.[40]
- According to the OECD, the United States ranks seventeenth in terms of public spending on primary and secondary education among OECD and partner nations.[41]

As argued earlier, underperforming students will become a net cost rather than a net contributor to our economy and society. If you doubt the economic impact of education on prosperity, just look at the results of the GI Bill introduced in America after the Second World War. "To illustrate the profound impact of the GI Bill one needs only recite the stark statistics: two years before the war approximately 160,000 U.S. citizens were in college. By 1950, the figure had risen to nearly 500,000. In 1942, veterans accounted for 49 percent of college enrollments."[42] For further evidence of the GI Bill's positive impacts, consider this: In *Over Here: How the GI Bill Transformed the American Dream* (Houghton Mifflin Harcourt, 2006), author Edward Humes wrote that the groundbreaking legislation made education possible for "fourteen future Nobel Prize winners, three Supreme Court justices, three presidents, a dozen senators, two dozen Pulitzer Prize winners, 238,000 teachers, 91,000 scientists, 67,000 doctors, 450,000 engineers, 240,000 accountants, 17,000 journalists, 22,000 dentists—along with a million lawyers, nurses, businessmen, artists, actors, writers, pilots, and others."

For a more current perspective, look at PISA's report "The High Cost of Low Educational Performance." It indicates that "A modest goal of having all

OECD countries boost their average PISA scores by 25 points over the next 20 years—which is less than the most rapidly improving education system in the OECD, Poland, achieved between 2000 and 2006 alone—implies an aggregate gain of GDP of US $115 trillion over the lifetime of the generation born in 2010."[43]

The dire case for education and the negative impacts on American competitiveness is more boldly pronounced in the Alliance for Excellent Education's report on the PISA study[44]:

The United States has substantial inequities in achievement . . . Moreover, the rapidly growing minority populations that represent a disproportionate share of America's lowest-achieving students are projected to make up more than half of the U.S. population by 2050 . . . Unless the United States begins to prepare all students for college and the modern workplace, America's disturbing downward trend will only get worse.

The following details how fifteen-year-old students from the United States compare with fifteen-year-olds in other OECD member countries in the Programme for International Student Achievement (PISA) measures of academic proficiency.

Reading Literacy

- In 2003, the United States ranked 15th of 29 OECD countries in reading literacy, and with a score of 495, coming in just below the OECD average of 500 (U.S. Department of Education, National Center for Education Statistics 2004). However, a printing error invalidated the U.S. reading section of the 2006 PISA assessment, so the current U.S. standing is unknown.

Scientific Literacy

- The United States ranks 21st of 30 OECD countries in scientific literacy, and the U.S. score of 489 fell below the OECD average of 500. [OECD, PISA 2006: Science competencies for tomorrow's world, 2007]
- One quarter (24.4 percent) of U.S. fifteen-year-olds do not reach the baseline level of science achievement. This is the level at which students begin to demonstrate the science competencies that will enable them to use science and technology in life situations. [OECD, PISA 2006]

Mathematics

- The United States ranks 25th of 30 OECD countries in mathematics literacy, and the average score of 474 fell well below the OECD average of 498. Scores have not measurably changed since 2003, when the United States ranked 24th of 29 countries. [OECD, PISA 2006]
- Over one quarter (28.1 percent) of American fifteen-year-olds performed below the baseline level of mathematics proficiency at which students begin to demonstrate the kind of skills that enable them to use mathematics actively in daily life. [OECD, PISA 2006]

Problem Solving

- In 2003, the U.S. ranked 24th of 29 OECD countries in problem solving, and the average score of 477 fell well below the OECD average of 500. [OECD, Problem solving for tomorrow's world: First measures of cross-curricular competencies from PISA 2003, 2004]
- Half of American students fell below the threshold of problem-solving skills considered necessary to meet emerging workforce demands. [OECD, Problem solving for tomorrow's world: First measures of cross-curricular competencies from PISA 2003, 2004] National surveys corroborate this finding; for example, 46 percent of American manufacturers say that their employees have inadequate problem-solving skills. [National Association of Manufacturers, The Manufacturing Institute, and Deloitte Consulting LLC, "2005 Skills Gap Report: A survey of the American manufacturing workforce," 2005]

The poor performance in math and science has broad-reaching effects on our higher education system. America has twenty-five of the top fifty universities in the world. How is it possible that the United States can have 50 percent of the world's finest universities and at the same time fail miserably in the education of its K–12 population? This is a question we cannot begin to answer fully in this book, but one factor is the influx of foreign students and professors.

In the critical subjects important to competitiveness and national security (engineering, mathematics, information systems, etc.), foreign students in American universities outnumber American students by three to one. Yet these students have no long-term allegiance to the United States, particularly after the USA Patriot Act of 2001.

We are training and in some cases financing our competition.

WHAT WE DON'T LEARN IN SCHOOL

If you believe we must find our way back to our values, then you cannot be happy with the fact that 95 percent of America's graduating high school seniors cannot give a basic account of American history. In 2010, the Goldwater Institute conducted a survey of 1,134 Arizona public high school students to test their civic knowledge. According to the Goldwater Institute, not a single student answered more than seven of the ten questions correctly. "Arizona high school students were recorded at a failure rate exceeding 96 percent."[45]

The problem does not end with elementary or high school students. In 2007, in a survey conducted by the Intercollegiate Studies Institute (ISI), 14,000 college students (7,000 freshmen and 7,000 seniors) at fifty colleges nationwide performed miserably on basic—but critical—history questions. The sixty-question, multiple-choice exam was designed to measure students' aptitude in four areas: basic American history, government, foreign affairs, and economics. The average score on the test was 50.4 percent for the freshmen and 54.2 percent for the seniors. ISI recently published the results of this survey in a report called, "The Shaping of the American Mind: The Diverging Influences of the College Degree and Civic Learning on American Beliefs."[46] In a companion study, in 2008 ISI administered a similar, shorter exam (thirty-three questions) to a random sample of 2,508 Americans in order to have a standard against which the impact of a college education on a threshold level of familiarity with basic American institutions could be determined.

Seventy-one percent of Americans failed this basic test. The overall average score was only 49 percent, with college graduates also failing at 57 percent.

The results of the studies reveal, at the very least, that Americans are not currently being and have not been educated in the basics of their own history, which parlays so critically into an embracing of this country's founding values. While one could make the argument that knowledge of history is not necessary to appreciate and practice the values on which this country lives, this argument is no different from claiming one can appreciate and practice healthy living without a basic knowledge of why and how the human body operates well. It is quite a stretch.

THE FOCUS ON WHAT WE'VE DONE WRONG

Imagine that you play football for Coach Vince Lombardi of the Green Bay Packers. He drives home one unchanging constant principle for his team: "Just win." This means no excuses, complaints, or explanations. Just win. But you understand that there are some firm, unchanging commitments necessary to attain such a level of excellence, and that once you embody the fundamental principle of winning it will take great discipline and vigilance to maintain it as the ethos of your being as a Green Bay Packer.

Suppose Americans saw America in the manner that Coach Lombardi sees his team: with imperfections, injuries, absences of talent here and there, but everyone committed to a single unchanging ideal?

Whatever the faults, misgivings, failures, and mendacities recorded in American history, America is distinct from other nations precisely because it is founded upon principles and values, not tradition and attritional change, and it is constantly on a path of exercising those principles and values in the hopes of cultivating a more perfect union.

It is important to teach critical thinking and to teach what has been, is, and may one day be wrong in or with America. But using America's past misdeeds, failings, and errors, both legal and moral, to teach and advance anti-Americanism undermines the very ideal, ethic, institutions, and values that created the country from which the student and the teacher have already benefited greatly. This practice simply should not be tolerated.

We will spend much more time exploring the role education can play in restoring America in part III, but here the point is that if we are not teaching our students what it means to be American, how can we expect them to fully commit and contribute to the American Experiment? The American Paradigm demands of us and locks us all into a certain discipline. That discipline is to understand and participate in the experiment and to advance the paradigm: our first principles and founding values and the spirit of the Lincoln Proposition. Neither propaganda misnamed as patriotism nor bitterness posing as radical critique gets us within the nearest limits of that discipline.

In America, our education should and must be designed (or redesigned) to teach and instill America's founding values, first principles, and its driving mechanism—the principles of gratitude, personal responsibility, and sacrifice, together with individualism. These unchanging values and principles constitute the very soul of what it means to be American and will see us to the ends of a more perfect union.

THE ROLE OF FAMILY IN EDUCATION

In his book *Outliers*, Malcolm Gladwell (following the work of psychologist Anders Ericsson) teaches us that it takes ten thousand hours to truly master anything. Interestingly, parents have almost exactly ten thousand waking hours with their children between birth and age three—that critical time neuroscientists tell us is the most crucial for brain development. This is the prime opportunity to begin to model and teach the values that will lay the foundation for thoughtful, active contributions to society later in life.

But consider the following facts from the A. C. Nielsen Company and ask yourself whether parents today are setting the right path: On average, parents spend only 3.5 minutes per week in meaningful discussions with their children. Two-thirds of infants and toddlers watch television, DVDs, or other types of video an average of two hours a day.[47]

If this nation is to attain the maximum potential of the development of human capital its freedoms allows, the role and function of parents should and must be to infuse the child's first ten thousand hours of life, when its capacity for absorption is at its apex, with the most comprehensive, unceasing attention possible, so that as that child grows, it will have obtained a foundation capable of motivating it toward a future based upon principles instilled by its parents rather than the disconnected and disconcerting array of a billion television episodes absorbed from the blur of celluloid.

Mr. Gladwell's "ten thousand hours" must be spent introducing, instilling, and reinforcing something. This reflects and establishes the role of parenting in the enterprise of nation building. The values of the home—respect, observance, obedience, duty, honor, and gratitude—are those that undergird and advance a nation built on individualism. What is needed in those ten thousand hours is not simply a constant repetition of those values, but activities, conversations, reviews of behaviors, and recognition that identifies, confirms, corrects, and rewards a child's progress toward those enduring principles of the home, which in so many ways are the foretelling of the character of the nation.

AMERICA IS A TIDE IN THE AFFAIRS OF MEN

Before we move forward, let us take a moment to reflect on all we have learned about where we are as a nation. America has been and is a force for good in the world. But when we reflect on the litany of evidence that the Paradox of Prosperity has taken hold, these revelations provide for us a clear picture of where and how our country can fail. This is not a screed about the failure of the American Experiment. And compared to many other nations, all is not bad for America, nor is all lost.

> *"Procrastination is still the thief of time . . . The 'tide in the affairs of men' does not remain at the flood; it ebbs. We may cry out desperately for time to pause . . . but time is deaf to every plea and rushes on. Over the bleached bones and jumbled residue of numerous civilizations are written the pathetic words: 'Too late.'"*
> —*Dr. Martin Luther King Jr.*

However, our question to ourselves must be this: With all we have heard and seen, all that is swirling around us, all that we know of the current situation here in America, are we not moving toward a "tipping point," as Malcolm Gladwell put it? Are we not approaching a moment in which even the greatest effort to change, reform, or save ourselves comes too late in our deterioration?

Is it possible to fall too far? As Dr. Martin Luther King Jr. said, "In this unfolding conundrum of life and history there is such a thing as being too late. Procrastination is still the thief of time. Life often leaves us standing bare, naked, and dejected with a lost opportunity. The 'tide in the affairs of men' does not remain at the flood; it ebbs. We may cry out desperately for time to pause in her passage, but time is deaf to every plea and rushes on. Over the bleached bones and jumbled residue of numerous civilizations are written the pathetic words: 'Too late.'"[48]

Our friends and enemies alike believe America is in decline. The financial facts of our situation and the changes in social attitudes and structures indicate a breakdown in the processes that seal a country together and ensure the transition of its values from generation to generation. We will have to rediscover our original American principles if we hope to restore America to its rightful place as the last best hope for mankind.

PART III

How:
What Americans Can
Do *for* America

It is said that circumstances don't make or break us; they reveal us. What is being revealed about America today? A generation from now, what will be said of what our country used to be? Will today's circumstances have produced a profound turning point or a perilous breaking point?

There is no doubt we are facing difficult times. There is also no doubt we have faced difficult times before. In fact, a brief review of American history will tell you the harshest circumstances of our past have played a prominent role in improving our future. Consider the progress spurred by the Civil War, the Great Depression, the civil rights era, and the Cold War.

Our past reveals we have largely allowed the furnace of adversity to melt away the dross from our democracy. America has repeatedly found a way to shine brighter on the other end.

We must find a way to shine brighter again.

We are not without hope in America. We never are, because the very mechanism with which our great country was founded has proven time and again to sustain us and take us to a higher plain. Our part is to once again place our fervent faith in our founding values and the core tenets of gratitude, personal responsibility, and sacrifice.

We have been given much. "When the architects of our republic wrote the magnificent words of the Constitution and the Declaration of Independence," asserted Dr. Martin Luther King Jr., "they were signing a promissory note to which every American was to fall heir. This note was the promise that all men, yes, black men as well as white men, would be guaranteed the unalienable rights of life, liberty and the pursuit of happiness."[49]

We are heirs to the greatest national freedoms the world has ever known. We must each, with our own means and in our own way, embrace our common inherited role.

"I have lived a long time," said Thomas Edison, "and I have seen history repeat itself again and again. I have seen many depressions in business. Always America has come out stronger and more prosperous. Be as brave as your fathers before you. Have faith. Go forward."

9

PERSONAL RESPONSIBILITY CAN COMBAT ENTITLEMENT

Anyone who trades liberty for security deserves neither liberty nor security.

—BENJAMIN FRANKLIN

If America is truly in decline and the American way of life—which has produced prosperity for so many—is now threatened, it is because we have ceased to create Americans with an abiding faith in our founding values. As a result, we have seen a slow and constant shifting and altering of those values to bring them in line with our prevalent behavior, rather than a constant and vigilant effort to bring our behavior closer to our founding values.

What happens when the principles that gave you all you possess eventually lead to distracting and damaging habits and attitudes that take you away from those principles and lead to the wasting away of prosperity? How do you combat the Paradox of Prosperity? Do you abandon those principles, or do you recommit to them through discipline?

Unlike other nations, which may try this or that ideology, America has a fixed foundation that allows for all of its political, economic, and social variety. In order to restore a sense of responsibility and obligation to ourselves, to our families, to our communities, and to our country, we must enter a process of reflection, restoration, and recommitment.

How do we do this?

There is no "quick fix," no eureka moment, though we wish there were one, given the rate of our apparent decline. Our current situation has been in the making for decades, as generations have watched and contributed to the very dire situation in which we now find ourselves. So the solution, like the problem, will take time, personal discipline, an extraordinary dedication of purpose, and constant vigilance. It will not be easy.

It will take coordinated and committed action akin to a battle plan to create Americans who, whether born here or naturalized, embrace and embody the founding values and the threefold mechanism for implementing those values: gratitude, personal responsibility, and sacrifice.

While a restoration of and return to our first principles and founding values through a stronger spirit of citizenship is the most logical path, clearly any solution will require political will and political action. Such political will and action can either come naturally and voluntarily from our national leaders—who recognize the crisis and embrace the critical need for the return to our founding values as the road map to take us out of our problems and into the future—or it can be thrust upon them by the voices, votes, and grassroots activism of a critical mass of concerned citizens. No matter which way unfolds, the future of America rests in one thing: our ability to recognize and admit the real cause of our decline and to make the necessary choices and sacrifices to restore our great nation.

Generally, only two things—inspiration or desperation—move people (or in this case, a nation) to make the kind of dramatic changes and sacrifices that will be necessary to change their dire circumstances. Enter the third, final part of this book with the following in mind: Given our economic and social situation, we will either take inspiration from the values that gave us so much or act on the desperation that befalls us because of our abandonment of those values.

Either way, the first step is to accept that each of us has a personal responsibility for restoring our nation if we want to continue to receive the benefits it offers. And that personal responsibility must be evident in our daily lives.

We must operate in a Triangle of Responsibility: This means first, developing a greater sense of personal responsibility in every American; second, limiting government; and third, limiting entitlements to the greatest extent possible. When we each take personal responsibility, the government can thus be limited because it must only perform its necessary functions. Entitlements are subsequently limited—as is the government's funding of them—because people are not relying on the government for things they can provide for themselves. This further ensures that the government remains limited and our freedoms remain exercisable. When all three points of the triangle are heeded, they operate in concert to naturally stabilize and stimulate not only the highest enjoyment of our freedoms but also the highest growth of our economy.

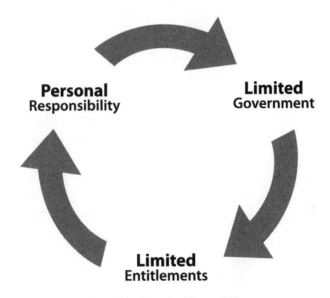

Figure 9.1—Triangle of Responsibility

PERSONAL RESPONSIBILITY

We must reposition ourselves toward our founding values. We must, in our everyday actions, project the responsibility we say we want to teach our young. Integrity demands it, prosperity requires it, and individualism cannot abide any other approach.

LIMITED GOVERNMENT

It follows naturally from our founding values that America must represent, fundamentally, a constant attempt to make all processes of government self-sufficient as often and as soon as possible.

What we are saying is that America, imagined rightly and behaving consistently with its values, will in every respect and for every purpose, as much as possible, undertake policies, enact legislation, or erect institutions the root aim of which is to reflect or support its values. So, for example, if a library is needed, the government should establish one. But it should be structured such that a "limiting rule" is its guiding spirit: As much and as soon as possible, local communities begin to act in their own interests and fund that library.

We are not suggesting that if a community cannot afford a library it should go without one. Rather, at the point at which resources are available for the library, the community should take over financial responsibility of that library.

If this ethic was prevalent in every policy in communities all over America, it would prevent the creeping osmosis by which the federal government "extends the hand" of the American taxpayer—in the generosity for which we are rightly heralded—only to find, decades later, that the helping hand has become a crutch upon which the beneficiaries continue to lean. This is "mission creep," and it is a fatal conceit to assume that we can undertake policy, enact legislation, or extend benefits without this limiting rule. It preserves our institutional integrity insofar as our values are concerned and preserves the pride of the beneficiary community when they become self sufficient, while also preserving the capacity of the government to extend a hand only when it leads to that sufficiency.

Again, applying our limiting rule, everything that the government does must only be done with the intention that the beneficiaries take over ultimate responsibility for themselves.

TEARING DOWN THE ENTITLEMENT APPARATUS

Entitlement is the antithesis of personal responsibility. We previously discussed the idea that one cannot be an individualist and retain a sense of entitlement. In fact, the very presence of the entitlement apparatus is anathema to America, a nation built on individualism that has at its very heart a deep-seated sense of personal responsibility.

A critical step in eradicating the attitude of entitlement must be the tearing down of the entitlement apparatus. Based on our founding values, there should be as little as possible named or arranged as an entitlement funded by government in America.

We have searched for politicians, economists, or commentators who could show a deep, meaningful understanding of our entitlement crisis. Among those who have made important contributions is Andrew Biggs of the American Enterprise Institute for Public Policy Research. In his March 2010 article "Entitlement Apocalypse," published by *National Review Online*, Mr. Biggs offered both an analysis of and an approach to reform that is impressive, effective, and would get this country closer to behaving according to its values.[50] His words on the subject of Social Security are profound, and he succinctly captures the problems inherent in each of our national entitlement programs:

> Social Security's costs are driven primarily by the effects of population aging on the program's pay-as-you-go financing, which redistributes taxes from workers as benefits to retirees. But Social Security's inability to save money is important as well: While the program has a $2.5 trillion trust fund, several econometric studies have shown that policymakers don't actually save its surpluses, but rather spend them or use them to finance tax cuts. As a result, future taxpayers will be no better off than they would have been had the trust fund never existed.
>
> In addition, Social Security paid extraordinarily high returns to early participants, a practice that prevented it from building savings that, had they actually been saved, would have helped it weather the looming demographic crisis. A typical individual retiring in 1965, for instance, received benefits amounting to eight times what he had paid in Social Security taxes. Earlier retirees did even better. Had these participants received only what they contributed, plus interest, the trust-fund balance would today be around $15 trillion higher . . .
>
> A Social Security program for the future must do three things: save more money, give people incentives to retire later in life, and target resources where they are needed most.
>
> First, everyone who can save for retirement on his own should do so.

President Obama and many Republicans support automatic enrollment in 401(k) and IRA pension plans. If all Americans saved just 10 percent of their wages, the need for Social Security payments would be greatly reduced. And, upon retirement, individuals should convert part of their savings to annuities; perhaps annuitized funds could be withdrawn tax-free while other withdrawals are taxed. For the typical person, these steps alone would accomplish most of what Social Security now achieves.

Second, able-bodied individuals should remain in the workforce longer. In the 1950s, the typical worker claimed Social Security around age 68. Today, despite a longer lifespan and work that is less physically demanding, the median American claims Social Security at age 62. It is an economic, budgetary, and moral mistake for Americans to spend one-third of their adult lives in retirement at the expense of those who work. The early and normal retirement ages for Social Security should be raised.

But we should use carrots as well as sticks. My research has shown that the typical worker nearing retirement age receives only around three cents in extra benefits for each additional dollar he pays into Social Security. To give this worker a good reason to keep working, the Social Security payroll tax should be reduced or eliminated for individuals older than 62.

Third, Social Security benefits for high earners should be reduced. While certain pundits object that "a program for the poor is a poor program"— a view based on the uncharitable assumption that if Americans know a program is redistributive, they won't support it—the current system gives about $27,000 per year in benefits to every retiree who earned more than $100,000 per year when working. This is a luxury a program facing insolvency cannot afford.

What we see here are two conservative principles in conflict with one another. On the one hand, Mr. Biggs clearly would not recommend redistributive policies. On the other hand, in his attempt to maintain the conservative principle of fiscal prudence, he is led to the threshold of a redistributive conclusion. I agree with Mr. Biggs that radical changes are necessary both in attitudes and in practice to reform the Social Security system. However, I believe in the principle of each according to his labor. I also believe that the best government is the least government. As such, I cannot accept that those who pay into the entitlement apparatus should see their returns in benefits lessen according to the government's calculus of who should benefit from what they have not contributed. Of course, to the degree that the system would provide benefits in excess of what the individual contributed (plus a modest rate of interest on that amount), I then would consider such benefits an entitlement that should not be supported.

Biggs continues:

> Social Security's benefit formula also needs repair. As my research has shown, most of the redistribution in Social Security is based on factors other than income. In fact, a worker's earnings level is a poor predictor of how generously Social Security will treat him. Single-earner couples do better than dual-earner couples; short working careers produce higher benefits than do longer ones; divorced women whose marriages lasted ten years or longer do better than those who divorced earlier. This means that some low-earning households receive relatively low benefits, while some high-earning households receive relatively generous ones. A flatter, simpler benefit structure would make Social Security more understandable and would more effectively prevent poverty . . .
>
> The experiences of other countries might teach us something. The United Kingdom is moving to increase its benefits, coupled with automatic enrollment in pension accounts. These accounts will invest an amount equal to 8 percent of workers' earnings, with contributions split between workers, employers, and the government. Australia requires all workers to save 9 percent of their wages in individual accounts; for low earners, it provides a minimum benefit.
>
> Meanwhile, New Zealand offers a flat universal benefit to all retirees, with voluntary "Kiwi Saver" retirement accounts providing additional income. Such a setup would be a significant change from our current system, but would allow us to give the household of every retired and disabled worker a poverty-level benefit with a payroll tax of under 6 percent. A reform that effectively eliminated poverty for retirees and generated income above the poverty level by means of individual savings would be good policy, and might even be good politics.
>
> Reforming Social Security is important not only for its own sake, but to

conserve resources for Medicare, where it will be harder to supplant dwindling government benefits with personal savings.

Medicare's fiscal challenge is like Social Security's on steroids. Medicare faces all of Social Security's demographic challenges, and also bears the burden that health expenditures have long been growing faster than the economy.

Medicare costs around $450 billion per year. That's a lot of money, but at least seniors are receiving better health care, right? Actually, it's far from clear. MIT's Amy Finkelstein and Wellesley's Robin McKnight found that Medicare raised seniors' hospital spending by 37 percent in its first ten years (it was created in 1965) without lowering their death rates. It is true that seniors who might otherwise have no insurance now benefit from Medicare, but we could cover them for a fraction of the current cost. Seniors who can afford their own insurance pay less out of pocket with Medicare, but their health isn't much better for it: When at age 65 they shift from private plans to Medicare, they experience no reduction in mortality.

In today's dollars, Medicare will spend $775 billion by 2020 and $1.4 trillion by 2030, according to Congressional Budget Office projections. But Medicare's problem isn't just rising costs; it's also that so much of what we spend is wasted. An entitlement program that refuses no qualified claim, pays on a fee-for-service basis, and charges low deductibles invites disregard for cost effectiveness.

To restrain the rise of costs, Medicare reimburses health-care providers at rates about 20 percent lower than those paid by private insurers. But to compensate, many providers simply conduct extra procedures, according to a recent Department of Health and Human Services study . . . A consumer-oriented approach might be a viable alternative. One such approach is "premium support": Medicare would provide each beneficiary a fixed supplement, adjusted for age, income, and health status. The Federal Employees Health Benefits Plan operates on this basis, with a government contribution set at 72 percent of the average premium. Using these funds, plus their own money, participants choose from up to two dozen providers.

Since consumers pay any premiums above the government share, and are free to choose between competing plans, they have an incentive to spend efficiently, which in turn gives providers an incentive to provide quality care at an affordable cost. The point of such a policy isn't to design and impose the best plan, but to create a market structure that will find the best plan by means of competition and innovation. And the best plan may not be the same for each person, which is another reason we should empower individuals to make their own health-care choices . . .

Increased Medicare efficiency would reduce the pain of the inevitable cuts in benefits. Medicare savings of even 10 percent would amount to $75 billion by 2020 and $135 billion by 2030. And other solutions are not presenting themselves.

That brings us to Medicaid, a means-tested state/federal program that provides health care to low-income and disabled individuals. Medicaid does not have a single structure; rather, each state runs its own program, consistent with certain federally imposed requirements, and decides how much to spend . . . In 2010, Medicaid spending will likely top $500 billion—even more than Medicare outlays—with costs split roughly 60-40 between Washington and the states. Medicaid is responsible for around 15 percent of all U.S. health-care spending, and is the biggest line item in state budgets.

Medicaid spending has grown—and, in consequence, crowded out private insurance—in part because of population aging and rising health-care costs, but also because states have significantly expanded eligibility in recent years [to population segments who may or may not need the benefit, particularly if they had saved over time to fund long-term care later in life]. And that is largely because such expansions bring more federal funds to their coffers.

The federal government covers 50 to 75 percent of Medicaid costs, depending on the state's average income. This means that the states can provide $2 to $4 in total benefits for each $1 they spend. Under such terms, even an obviously wasteful benefit extension makes budgetary sense from the state's perspective. And cuts work the same way: Paring Medicaid spending by $4 million would save Mississippi only $1 million, while New York must cut $2 million to save $1 million. The result is a ratchet effect whereby costs increase in good times when the states can spend more on it and hold steady in bad times when states reduce funding for it.

The matching formula also skews Medicaid resources from poor states to rich ones, since only the rich can afford to run large Medicaid programs.

As with Medicare, the key to reforming Medicaid is shifting

incentives—this time, for state lawmakers. A modest but helpful change would be simply to reduce matching rates as Medicaid spending rises, so that if states choose to expand Medicaid into the middle class they must bear the cost themselves.

A farther-reaching reform would be to fund Medicaid through block grants to the states while expanding the states' flexibility with regard to program design. (A similar approach was part of the 1996 welfare reform.) If a state wished to expand Medicaid beyond what the block grant paid for, it would have to do so with its own dollars. [This applies our "limiting rule," forcing beneficiaries to take responsibility and requiring state politicians, policy makers, and local voters to take responsibility for their decisions rather than spreading that responsibility to the national government and the nation as a whole.]

All Americans should save for their own retirement and health-care needs. Only those whose savings are insufficient should receive supplements. Innovation, competition, and choice, which make American consumer markets the most vibrant in the world, should play a central role. Entitlement-reform policy isn't much more complicated than that.

What is so intriguing about Mr. Biggs's proposals is that they primarily rest on "incentive shifting" and on the idea that each individual and policy maker should exhibit personal responsibility, and in so doing, our entitlement problems would be dramatically reduced. Yet if you search for proposals or initiatives that reflect serious efforts to bring America back to financial and economic health by reducing entitlement spending, embarrassingly, you will find few. And you will find even fewer leaders who are showing intellectual honesty about our problems and radical change—the type of change we need.

In 2005, Representative Jeb Hensarling and fifty-eight other representatives introduced H.R. 2290, legislation that would dramatically change budget rules and procedures. While there were a number of provisions in the legislation, a cornerstone was the implementation of caps on nondefense discretionary spending that would require deep cuts in most entitlement programs (Social Security was untouched). The Congressional Budget Office assessed the required savings—through reductions in spending—if legislation similar to Hensarling's proposal were to pass, and this is what it would have looked like by 2016:

Entitlement Reductions over Ten Years if Congress Cut All Entitlements Proportionately in Response to Entitlement Caps

Medicare	$919 billion
Medicaid	$460 billion
Federal civilian retirement and disability	$127 billion
Military retirement and disability	$74 billion
Unemployment compensation	$73 billion
Earned income and child tax credits	$72 billion
Supplementary security income	$69 billion
Veterans benefits	$56 billion
Food stamps	$54 billion
TANF and other family support	$37 billion
Child nutrition	$25 billion
Commodity Credit Corporation price supports	$21 billion
TRICARE for life	$16 billion
Other federal retirement and disability	$15 billion
Foster care and adoption assistance	$13 billion
Student loans	$13 billion
Universal Service Fund	$11 billion
State Children's Health Insurance Program	$8 billion
Social services (Title XX, voc rehab)	$7 billion
Other miscellaneous	$22 billion
Total	**$2,092 billion**

If Hensarling's legislation had passed, we would be into the fifth year, well on our way to savings of $2.1 trillion. Those savings would eventually reduce our national debt and be put back in the pockets of individuals and small businesses, helping to offset the critical economic challenges we currently face. But of course, this legislation did not pass. Politicians in both parties, for the most part, make decisions that are expedient and that will help ensure re-election. Even Hensarling's proposal did not address the issues with Social Security. Why? Likely because older people are diligent voters.

So how can we affect national policy in these areas?

Let's be frank: There are only small ways in which individual Americans can move the entitlement reform debate, specifically as it relates to Social Security, Medicare, and Medicaid. And as it turns out, most of the actions likely to have a direct impact are driven by personal choice and personal responsibility.

1. Citizens must vote. They must vote for politicians who are committed to reform and unafraid of the consequences of doing what's right. Ultimately, it is going to take politicians to make the changes to our entitlement apparatus. Of course, finding politicians who are willing to make these tough decisions and ultimately cast their votes are hard to come by, but we must search for those committed to our founding values and we must vote.

   As said above, Andrew Biggs made an excellent proposal. Yet no politician on any side of the political divide has embraced it or any portion of it as a path to a policy. We noted that Representative Hensarling proposed legislation, but it never fully addressed the reform question. Why is that? Because politicians will not risk advancing an idea of reform that calls for real sacrifice if they feel they will not be reelected. For this reason, the first thing the average American can do is to let politicians know that it is all right to reform Social Security and other entitlements, and that all cards should be on the table. This alone gives us the very best chance to advance the discussion of reform.

   While it is a discussion for another day, I believe that term limits would immediately change the environment in Washington, and what would otherwise be difficult (and even political suicide) would become much easier as the hope of a "lifetime position" would no longer be on politicians' minds.

2. Specific groups can do more. Consider this from a more recent paper by Mr. Biggs: "Population aging is easily understood: the baby-boomer generation is retiring, seniors are living longer, and smaller families leave fewer workers to support them. The ratio of workers to beneficiaries, which is now over 3 to 1, will fall to almost 2 to 1 in 2035. Aging alone will ultimately raise entitlement costs by nearly 50 percent in coming decades."[51]

It follows from this that the specific group that has real power to influence politicians is the baby boomers, who are near or at retirement age. But why should people who are the immediate beneficiaries of a system act to change that system, potentially lessening in the process the cash value of benefits they may receive?

The answer is really simple: Either we are responsible or we are not. But I believe if we are intellectually honest in our discussions with near-retirees and retirees, they will both listen and respond favorably.

But can they have a real impact?

It turns out the answer is yes!

Consider this: "Health care costs are rising for three reasons. First, as incomes rise, the value of health increases relative to other goods. Second, technology generates treatments we gladly would have purchased in the past, but could not since they did not yet exist. Today they exist and we buy them. Third, [this is the more significant reason why that "yes" is possible] the falling share of health care paid out-of-pocket—from 47 percent in 1960 to 12 percent today—*encourages patients to purchase even marginally useful treatments, since they are mostly spending other people's money*" (emphasis added).[52]

Now here is the impact individuals can have by taking responsibility for their health care, by making responsible choices that are motivated—dare I say—by gratitude for all that this nation has done for them, and by making a small sacrifice, each according to his capacity, to exercise fiscal prudence in a time of crisis.

The effects of these options are difficult to quantify, but the RAND Corporation health experiment of the 1970s and '80s found that working-age individuals who paid 25 percent of health costs out-of-pocket spent around 20 percent less than those with no cost sharing. Individuals with the equivalent of health savings accounts spent around 30 percent less.

3. Working-age individuals should pay more of their health care costs out-of-pocket in order to save the system and to give politicians a green light on reform. According to Mr. Biggs's analysis, this may even save them money. We know it will discipline the other expenditures and force upon them a financial prudence that the culture of

entitlement has undermined in our personal financial decisions, as Mr. Biggs himself shows.

Near-retirees and retirees can take the options we proposed above and preserve their individual choice to delay, transfer, or take their benefits in kind, as a means of both contributing to our fiscal well-being and taking personal responsibility.

I believe if these few measures were undertaken, it would embolden politicians to take the intellectually honest approach to reforming Social Security and our health care entitlement apparatus. Those who are in need would benefit, and those with means would, by choice, contribute further to aid their fellow Americans. The country would benefit in two further ways: First, these actions would stop the "rot" and move the discussion on reform to an honest plane, which is good for our democracy. And second, it would demonstrate—to ourselves, our children, and the world—the power of gratitude and how it motivates sacrifice; that Americans are capable of making the difficult decisions necessary to put right a system that has gone badly wrong. In a triumph of reform, citizens would restore the principle that the people govern and the government serves.

10

NATIONAL SERVICE CAN TEACH GRATITUDE AND SACRIFICE

The consideration that human happiness and moral duty are inseparably connected will always continue to prompt me to promote the former by inculcating the practice of the latter.

—GEORGE WASHINGTON

The spirit of gratitude and sacrifice is essential to all relationships of respect and honor. Every society is either moving toward an increase in honor and grace in the relationships among individuals, between individuals and their communities, and between individuals and their nation . . . or it is decaying.

What does that decay look like in daily life?

One poignant example is when soldiers risk their lives—or as Lincoln said at Gettysburg, give their "last full measure of devotion"—to protect our national values, while that nation's citizens engage in trivial pursuits, showing neither respect nor gratitude for those men and women whose lives are being laid on the line. Such a nation will not long be able to count on the sacrifices of those noble individuals to maintain the freedoms and prosperity it enjoys.

How do we imbue our culture with a renewed sense of gratitude and sacrifice?

We must understand and develop a means to ingrain the reciprocal structure of these two values so common citizens exemplify them every day. And then we must model them and require them through a national program that grows the American spirit in every future generation.

THE CYCLE OF GRATITUDE AND SACRIFICE

There are those who feel, adopt, sacrifice, and exhibit gratitude organically. These are not innate values, however, and most people must learn them. But how?

There is a simple, elegant, circular structure inherent in the nature of sacrifice and gratitude: sacrifice begets gratitude, which begets sacrifice. So the best way to teach these two attributes is to exhibit them.

What does that cycle of sacrifice and gratitude look like in daily life?

Respect and honor should be built into our thinking, our words, and our actions toward parents, toward contributing members of our communities, toward those who sacrifice for us, and toward the ideal of a country from which we have received more benefits and prosperity than we could possibly earn.

RECOGNIZING SACRIFICES FOR OUR WAY OF LIFE

The communities we live in or hope for in America are possible only because of the sustained body of sacrifices chosen and embraced and even thrust upon those now serving us in numerous capacities and those who have served before. The recognition of these sacrifices is critical to our self-understanding; it is also requisite if we hope to cultivate the right motivation in those who may be called upon now and those on whose service we must depend in the future. One needs simply to fly into Washington over Arlington National Cemetery and see the graves of those who made the ultimate sacrifice. We must recognize these sacrifices meaningfully, conceptually, and constantly in order to create the possibility of a true gratitude for them.

Any nation in which Pat Tillman—who gave up fame and fortune as a star NFL player to sacrifice for his country by serving in the Airborne Rangers—pays the ultimate price, yet the media spends more time discussing Lindsay Lohan's latest display of self-centeredness, is a nation that cannot hold its prosperity for long. Why, you ask? Because such a nation cannot motivate those who give of themselves to defend that prosperity. This was the fate of the Roman Empire and it might be our fate should we continue on this path.

Put starkly, we cannot sustain a nation in which one group of people dies for our freedom while most of the rest of the population engages in self-indulgent behavior that undermines respect for the sacrifices made for that freedom. It is repugnant to the individualist ethic and every principle America was built upon, not least of which is that we pay for every detriment met by others on our behalf, even if that payment in a given moment is simply recognition and respect.

We are inoculated against and sequestered from the conflicts in which our soldiers fight because they don't affect our daily lives—or so we believe. We shop as others sacrifice; go to the movies while others sacrifice. We work or don't, contribute to our communities or don't—all while others sacrifice. Yet we rely on their sacrifices and the nonmilitary sacrifices of so many others so that we can live our lives as we please. And if the majority of our citizens are never in a position to make sacrifices, even less extreme ones, or are not even aware of the sacrifices being made every day on their behalf, we cannot maintain our prosperity, power, or prestige in the world.

Think about the First and Second World Wars. During those conflicts, communities organized to support our troops and our nation. Many women worked in factories making equipment for the war. Others organized to collect and send support packages to our troops. Blacks enlisted and served, even though they did not enjoy full-scale liberty at home. In spite of his anger about the condition of blacks, W.E.B. Du Bois, the great scholar and sociologist, supported the involvement of the United States in the First World War. Breaking with the editors of other African-American journals, he wrote in an editorial in *The Crisis*: "Let us not hesitate. Let us, while this war lasts, forget our special grievances and close our ranks shoulder to shoulder with our own white fellow citizens."[53]

In an article entitled "The Act of Remembering Grows Patriotism" in the *San Antonio Express-News* (May 30, 2010), Maj. Gen. Patrick Brady, U.S. Army (retired)—who was awarded the Medal of Honor for heroism in Vietnam—explains the importance of gratitude: "The great thing about our beloved dead is they never really die as long as we remember. The noblest part of their being remains with us . . . everywhere in this great land, a part of our common ideals and feeling for each other, of all those things that make us a united country."[54]

Regardless of one's views concerning the correctness or legitimacy of the policy decisions, our citizens must have a clear idea and parents must ensure that children know and understand what sacrifices have been and are being made for the sake of the freedoms we enjoy.

CITIZENS MCCAIN AND STOCKDALE

I want to share with you a story about someone most of you already know— U.S. Senator and former presidential candidate John McCain.

Senator McCain's service exemplifies the type of sacrifice for country that we seem to have forgotten and that we desperately need to instill in our young people. Regardless of how you feel about Senator McCain's politics, it is important to grasp deeply the meaning such an American brings to the concept of sacrifice. His story of personal cost and suffering should remind us of a patriotism that lies beyond partisan punditry and name-calling for expedient political points.

Senator McCain was a fighter pilot in the U.S. Navy, and on October 26, 1967, he was shot down while on a bombing mission over Hanoi during the Vietnam War. He ejected from his plane, breaking both arms and a knee in the process. He landed in Truc Bach Lake and was hauled from the water by North Vietnamese citizens, who began to beat him, kick him, spit on him, and stab him. They broke more bones. The Viet Cong arrived, put him on a stretcher, and delivered him to the Hao Lo prisoner of war camp—called the Hanoi Hilton by POWs—where he was kept in horrific conditions.

Amazingly, he did not die. Nine months later, he was still in that prison when his situation changed for the worse, as he described in his autobiography, *Faith of My Fathers* (Perennial, 2000):

> In mid-June 1968, the camp commander, over an inviting spread of biscuits and cigarettes, asked me if I would like to go home . . . my father had become Commander in Chief, Pacific. The Vietnamese intended to hail his arrival with a propaganda spectacle, releasing his son as a gesture of "goodwill." I

wanted to say yes: I was tired and sick and I was afraid. But the Code of Conduct was explicit: "American prisoners cannot accept parole or amnesty or special favours." I said I would think about it . . .

For almost two months, nothing happened. Then the punishment sessions began. I was hauled into an empty room and kept there for four days. At intervals, the guards returned to administer beatings . . . They cracked several of my ribs and broke a couple of teeth . . . On the third night I lay in my blood and waste, so tired and hurt that I could not move. Three guards lifted me to my feet and gave me the worst beating yet. They left me lying on the floor moaning from the stabbing pain in my re-fractured arm.

While this story is almost too horrific to read, one can only imagine how much worse it must have been to live through. Now imagine how devastating it must be to an American who made this level of sacrifice to see the ordinary, daily disregard for the ideals for which he suffered so greatly. Yet what is most impressive is the sense of honor in the way Senator McCain refers to his experience.

We were told to have faith in God, country, and one another. Most of us did. But the last of these—faith in one another—was our final defense, the ramparts our enemy could not cross. This was the faith I had embraced at the Naval Academy. It was my father's and grandfather's faith. In prison, a filthy, crippled, broken man, all I had left of my dignity was the faith of my fathers. It was enough.

We live in a country that from its beginning required, was structured upon, and can only be advanced by citizens who are prepared to make the ultimate sacrifice to maintain our values and our freedoms. Both this sacrifice and the response of citizens through an active gratitude are a truer form of patriotism than pundits screaming at each other about who loves America more.

Another powerful example of such sacrifice is one so harrowing and, without a hint of embellishment, so unwelcome in the human imagination, one instantly feels a debt of gratitude and obligation at its telling. Vice Adm.

John Stockdale was held for more than seven years as a captive during the Vietnam War and experienced brutal torture.

Stockdale ejected from his plane, breaking his back and his leg in the process. He landed in a small village and was captured immediately. He was brutally beaten until the police came and hauled him away. He was brought to a prisoner camp where he lay on a ping-pong table for a month. Eventually, a doctor came and drained pus that was accumulating in his leg and then brought him to the hospital, where they worked with him until he was able to get around on crutches. Once he could, he was shipped back to the prison camp to face more torture, which he recounts in his autobiography *In Love and War* (Harper & Row, 1984):

> They got a couple of teams of torture guards and they had a special procedure. And the way it was done was to get a long iron bar and shackle your legs to it, and then the man on the back would start weaving ropes through your arms to bend them backwards. And then they—getting as much leverage as he could—what they're doing is shutting off the blood circulation in your upper body. And then he would push, he would bend you double and stand on your back and he would pull from this angle, giving him better leverage, and then he would find—you know it's about over when you feel the heel of his foot in . . . [the] back of your head and he put your nose right on the cement and there you are. You're encased in ropes. Your blood is not circulating. You're in pain and you're in claustrophobia.

Of his more than seven years in captivity, four were spent in solitary confinement.

One of the most highly decorated officers in American military history, Admiral Stockdale also happened to be a philosopher who could shed light on his experience through analysis and reflection. Through his reflections, we see an attitude that has been lost in the American spirit of citizenship. He shared his beliefs about personal responsibility and integrity in the face of harrowing tyranny, torture, and inhumanity:

> "What is the fruit of your doctrines?" someone asked Epictetus. "Tranquility, fearlessness, and freedom," he answered. You can have these only if you

are honest and take responsibility for your own actions. You've got to get it straight! You are in charge of you . . . I'm talking about having looked over the brink, and seen the bottom of the pit, and realizing the truth of that linchpin of Stoic thought: that the thing that brings down a man is not pain but shame!

Epictetus also said, "The lecture-room of the philosopher is a hospital; students ought not to walk out of it in pleasure, but in pain." Stockdale wrote, "If Epictetus's lecture room was a hospital, my prison was a laboratory—a laboratory of human behavior. I chose to test his postulates against the demanding real-life challenges of my laboratory." Stockdale epitomizes indomitable resolve—the refusal to define himself and his chances by the situation he was in—a resolve not unlike that which is required for leadership, crisis management, and general personal integrity.

In 1992, when Stockdale was candidate for vice president on Ross Perot's independent ticket, he received unfortunate treatment by the press. His television presentation proved difficult because he could not hear very well, and he was criticized as being too old, too doddering. But to paraphrase Dennis Miller's famous defense of Stockdale, the reason he could not hear is that his eardrum was busted for the sake of the very people who proceeded to disparage him as old and decrepit.

I am grateful to Senator McCain and Admiral Stockdale for enduring still more mental anguish in recounting their experiences as prisoners of war. Their stories are another gift they've presented this nation. For, as Alexander Solzhenitsyn—an equally venerable man who suffered for his beliefs— warned, it is dangerous for a nation to amputate its memory, for silent generations to grow old and die without ever talking about themselves, either to each other or to their descendants. And so what is most important this day is that our youth see that we remember, that we are grateful, and that service and sacrifice and courage are noble things.

To promote our values, America has required and produced great personalities in every area of human endeavor. The greatest personalities, in my view, are those who are prepared to lay down their lives for our republic. This sort of commitment is the antithesis of the attitude of entitlement and the culture of complaint. From the study of these personalities, we can, simply by reading a book, witness and reconfirm the spirit, valor, and daring it takes to keep a nation safe and strong. Here, among these brave and tireless ones, there is no complaint, no sense of entitlement, and no expectation of reward. How ironic that we can live in a nation whose freedom has been secured by people of this sort of courage without complaint, for the sake of other people who seem to complain bitterly and endlessly, even when their troubles are mostly of their own making.

If you are asking what you can take from the lives of Senator McCain, Admiral Stockdale, and others like them, it is this: There is a line of connection that must be maintained between those who pay or risk paying the ultimate price for our nation's safety, freedom, and prestige and those who benefit from their sacrifice. We cannot have a situation where there is not a scintilla of the fiber exhibited by those who make the sacrifice in the mind, body, and spirit of those who benefit from it. And those of us who benefit, if we are truly grateful for those sacrifices, must resolve to keep an awareness of what has been laid down for us, and ask ourselves continually this question: In what way does my life, in some aspect, reflect and commemorate the sense of honor and the dignity of those who risk and pay the ultimate sacrifice for my life in the first place? This is how sacrifice and gratitude binds us in citizenship.

> *"Ask not what your country can do for you but what you can do for your country."*
> —John F. Kennedy

So ask yourself, what was the last sacrifice you made for your community or for your country? What have you done to promote our core values, to make our nation stronger?

"Ask not what your country can do for you but what you can do for your country."

THE RESTORATIVE GRATITUDE OF IMMIGRANTS

There is an old saying that groups, clubs, and opportunities are preserved by the last to gain entry. In this way, immigrants to America are the best, most immediate way to observe what America—the America we often take for granted—means to those who find the chance to become their best selves here.

For the Leiden Pilgrims, who arrived in America in 1620, the dominant emotional response to this land was, speaking generally, gratitude for escape from the travails of Holland and England. Here, they were not caught between the equally unwelcome oppositions of indentured servitude or monarchial tyranny.

Since that time, immigrants have come to America and immediately become beneficiaries of the liberty and protection of their pursuit of happiness. Historian and professor Simon Scharma wrote in *The American Future* (HarperCollins, 2009):

> Now why, then, should a man remain in the social prisons of European tradition? Why would anyone with a grain of commonsense or self-respect feel attachment to the accidental geography of his nativity, for "a country that had no bread for him, whose fields procured for him no harvest, who met with nothing but frowns of the rich, the severity of the laws, with jails, punishments, who owned not a single foot of the extensive surface of the planet?" To leave such vexation behind was to experience social rebirth.[55]

The immigrants who arrive in our country reap benefits they could not earn at home. The liberties and prosperity that America offers those it welcomes and absorbs are the results of sacrifices of those already here and those who have come before. But more than that, the principles and values of this nation and the sacrifices that secured them deliver more than any immigrant could possibly give in exchange for an invitation to become an American.

And yet a person sitting somewhere today, in a land with another set of values, longs for his invitation.

Because of the sacrifices that have been made, the immigrant is prepared to do whatever is necessary in hopes of adding her story to the stories of those who have "made it" here. She appreciates her entry, and, motivated by all this nation bequeaths her upon citizenship, she insists upon sacrifice. My grandfather once told me of my great-grandparents' first step off the boat at Ellis Island in 1903. My great-grandfather knelt to the ground, pressed his face to the soil, and kissed it. He and my great-grandmother had only twenty dollars to their name for their entire family of five, yet they were abundantly grateful for their newfound freedom and the opportunity to make something beautiful of their lives. This they did.

What is the attractive power of America? Why do and why would so many risk so much to be here? If we reflect on the wealth created by America's values of personal responsibility, sacrifice, and gratitude—together with individualism—or if we ponder deeply the Lincoln Proposition that in America, "The man who labored for another last year, this year labors for himself, and next year he will hire others to work for him," we can understand how and why America attracts people from every nation in the world. Our attractive power, quite simply, rests in our values: That all men are created equal and are thus endowed by our Creator with inalienable rights. No power on Earth can alter these rights, which are protected by law, enacted by those who govern with the consent of the governed.

What has this produced? Only the greatest prosperity and degree of protected liberty, for the largest number of people, known to human history. This prosperity and liberty are open to all in America. Each person may test himself against the possibility that he can improve his lot in life according to his own interest, effort, and resources.

Fortified by the rewards of their own efforts, immigrants come to know the meaning of America and become standard bearers of the American values. They impart to their children what lies in wait for them, in a world their parents could never have imagined. They know now—perhaps more readily than natural-born citizens—the extent of the American values. They come to appreciate living in liberty as part of those who consent to be governed and protected by the rule of law, which has been secured by those who have given the "last full measure of devotion."

The immigrant arrives in America "in arrears," indebted already for the sacrifices paid by others in our nation's history. So, if the immigrant is going to adopt the values of America, his first instinct must be gratitude. But how is that to be exhibited?

Upon becoming an American citizen, the immigrant is asked to adopt and adapt to American values. As you read in chapter 2 in the section "Being American, Living the Paradigm," each immigrant is asked to accept the proposition of the motto on the official American seal, *e pluribus unum*, "out of many, one." This motto symbolizes the invitation into an ideal based on family-like values rather than cultural protocol. Across the globe, humanity, being unable to advance one culture above others, often resorts to posturing, shows of strength, and actual violence. They demand that those too weak to defend themselves admit the inferiority of their cultures.

But not in America.

And for this immigrants are grateful. Their gratitude spurs them on to make sacrifices for our country. Regardless of the political debates about immigration, neither our motto nor the important role of immigrants in our citizenry can be denied.

Therefore, it is curious that queries such as whether immigrants should learn to speak English have flourished. Of course the immigrant should learn English. Mere gratitude should motivate him to do that. But since America is "many" and "one," we should also welcome those of other languages and cultures to cultivate and share their languages and cultures, as it enriches the fabric of American life.

"Out of many, one" means that we can remain the many, but through acknowledgment, understanding, and appreciation of American values—first and foremost—we become one beautifully diverse family.

ALL WHO CAN MUST SERVE

Ambassador Adlai Stevenson once said, "What do we mean by patriotism in the context of our times? . . . What we mean is a sense of national responsibility . . . a patriotism which is not short, frenzied outbursts of emotion, but the tranquil and steady dedication of a lifetime. The dedication of a lifetime— these are words that are easy to utter, but this is a mighty assignment. For it is often easier to fight for principles than to live up to them."[56]

This is the meaning of patriotism—patriotism that is necessary for a nation such as America, with all of its obligations to its citizens and its challenges in the world. "Talking patriotism" will not do. What this nation cannot survive is the American who sees the chief responsibility of being American as merely the expression of opinions without repercussion rather than as the active assumption of certain duties.

In order to maintain this nation and its values, its citizens must have some mechanism through which to learn about the values that make them citizens. We need some mechanism through which to transfer to our young citizens a common thread of gratitude and sacrifice and what it means to be an American, and at the same time to ensure that everyone capable serves the nation in some capacity.

Therefore, I believe every able-bodied young person from the age of eighteen and every immigrant should perform at least one year of national service. I believe such service should be compulsory.

In August 2007, *Time* magazine ran a special series called "A Time to Serve: The Case for National Service." In that series, fundamental and compelling arguments were made for national service.

While it is not being proposed here, some have made the case for a national draft. It is believed by some military officers responsible for training the nation's forces, as well as by some politicians, that if there were a national draft, politicians would be less likely to wander off into meaningless conflicts, wasting American material and mortal treasure. The reason, as Representative Charles Rangel, a veteran and war hero, puts it is if you know your child may be sent off to war, you are likely to demand to know the reasons for the war and to apply the Powell Doctrine: Know what your objectives and exit strategies are before you go in. Define your success. Go in with overwhelming force. Get out once your objective is complete.

However, the military would rather have an all-volunteer military because they believe non-voluntary fighting personnel do not make the best soldiers. In the *Time* article series, Mark Thompson wrote a passage that highlights a practical point: "Many experts say that the sharp edge of today's volunteer military ... can only be dulled by adding draftees to the force. Most agree that any military obligation could be made more palatable if it were part of a bigger national-service program ... Those fulfilling their national-service obligation by enlisting would do so ... voluntarily (because they could [have chosen to serve] ... in some non-military slot)."[57]

Virtually no one is opposed to some sort of national service. And more importantly, as every nationalized immigrant must pledge to lay down his life for the country,[58] so should every native-born American at some point in his or her life. But I am not arguing for a national draft, and I don't believe national service men and women should be considered for combat service, except by choice.

The objective would be mandatory national service—which would include a period of basic training provided by the military—with an option for voluntary entrance into the military as one of many ways to fulfill a national service requirement. This allows everyone to serve, yet preserves the voluntary nature of the armed services. And, through the mandatory basic training portion of the program and subsequent service, young people are brought into close proximity to those who serve professionally so that politicians considering war will have to face a more engaged, educated citizenry—one that understands and appreciates the sacrifices made by those who serve and the human cost of involvement in military conflicts.

The spirit of community and support that emerged during the First and Second World Wars, in which almost everyone was involved, demonstrated to the world our resolve and our resilience. While we are not presently in a world war, our nation is "engaged" all across the globe, and we face a constant threat both from nations and from ideologies that would most certainly bring grave harm to America if they could do so. We must have a citizenry that is equally engaged and trained, paradigmatically unified, and ready to assist in times of emergency—whether a natural disaster or an attack on our homeland.

There are profound benefits to the program I propose, not least of which is a greater understanding among young people that there is a living thing called "the republic," which represents something for their own lives and for humanity. Other benefits include the following:

- A deep understanding of and gratitude for the sacrifices that others make for our country and a greater willingness to continue to make sacrifices throughout one's life
- A greater understanding, even if only in a limited way, of the meaning of service
- Bringing together young people of all classes, races, and ethnicities around a common goal
- The development of a unifying civic virtue—that liberty is preserved by those who act to secure it
- Cultivation of common understanding of national purpose
- Cultivation of empathy for and with nonpolitical national priorities
- Increased tolerance across political divides and social strata
- Greater personal investment in America's national purpose
- Friendships and bonds of respect
- A larger portion of the population with a clearer view than they generally have today of their role in the country

- The production of a limited but potent and potentially powerful citizenship network of people—a National Service Corps—who are determined to see their government uphold the duties and integrity of public office because they have a personal stake in those duties by virtue of service to their country
- Development of a sense of patriotism as defined previously
- A fit society, free from the debilitating effects of obesity and the associated health care costs

EXAMPLES FROM ABROAD

The national service systems of other countries (see the table that follows) can give us some insights into how such a program may be organized and what it could entail.

Foreign Examples of National Service Programs

Country	Eligible Citizens	Combat Expected	Exempt Service Tax
Singapore	ALL MEN—It is compulsory for all fit and able-bodied Singaporean men who have reached 18 years of age and are not deferred for certain reasons to be enlisted in military service or full-time national service (NSF). Singapore's military is a "total population source" militia. At any given time, Singapore can turn its entire citizenry into a martial force for the defense of the homeland.	YES—Upon completion of training, citizens attain an operationally ready date (ORD). Most NSF men will have to go through a 10-year cycle of military training with their assigned unit.	NO
Switzerland	ALL MEN—Switzerland has a militia and regular army. Only 5 percent of the militia is made up of professional soldiers; the rest are conscript citizens 18 to 34 years old.	NO—Switzerland being a neutral country, its army does not take part in armed conflicts in other countries.	YES—People unfit for service are exempted but pay a 3 percent additional annual income tax until the age of 30, except those with disability.

Israel	ALL NON-ARAB CITIZENS— National military service is mandatory for any non-Arab Israeli male or female citizen (as well as for Druze men) over the age of 18, although exceptions may be made on religious, physical, or psychological grounds. The Israel Defense Force (IDF) differs from most in the world in that it conscripts women.	YES—After completion of service, IDF may call up men as reservists one month yearly, up to age 45, or for active duty immediately in times of crisis.	NO

One interesting aspect of the Singapore model is that it provides a means of raising a total population source militia in the event of crisis. It further provides that every able-bodied male must enter a "battle ready" fitness regimen. The emphasis of Singapore's system is that in times of crisis, the whole citizenry can move into action. Similarly, Americans, from the age of eighteen, must become the repository of our homeland defense and disaster readiness—well trained, fit, aware, confident, and competent.

Likewise, in the Swiss model, all male citizens must enter training. Even naturalized males, once they obtain Swiss citizenship, must enter. The Swiss also have an interesting idea for those who are unable to serve for some reason other than disability. If they are gainfully employed they pay an "exemption fee" annually for ten years.

In Israel, everyone, males and females, goes through basic training. I believe it is important in the cultivation of a common understanding of the defense of the nation for everyone to gain some insight into what it must take to live in conditions more severe than are experienced in daily life, in defense of the freedoms all Americans enjoy.

There are other countries with versions of mandatory national service for nonmilitary purposes. Malaysia has a noncombat national service. And in Germany, the national service (noncombat) has proved so useful that an attempt to remove the mandatory requirement was defeated by hospitals and other social services agencies that have come to rely upon the country's national service corps.

What these countries show is that freedom is preserved by the participation of citizens. We cannot hold on to a republic based on the consent of the governed when those who must give that consent cannot conceive of or understand the reasons for the defense of the republic based on the values upon which it was founded.

THE MODEL OF THE SERVICE

I will not attempt to detail every aspect of a potential national service program but will provide a broad outline, based on proposals by others and research into successful programs in other countries. Note again that the following applies to all who are able to serve. There should be exemptions only for those whose physical or mental condition does not allow for participation. And those people should play whatever role is possible.

BASIC TRAINING AND PATRIOTIC EDUCATION

Six months is spent at either a military training facility or a local National Guard facility completing the following training programs:

Basic Training	This should entail the basic training that recruits receive in the military, including fitness, self-defense, and firearms training. It should include high-level physical challenges.
Survival & Disaster Training	This would entail dealing with disaster and relief operations and learning basic survival skills.
Life Saving Training	Participants would learn first aid, swimming, rescue, and basic firefighting.
Homeland Security	Service men and women can become assets in the case of any risk to the homeland, even if not part of the military service. Participants would learn how to support first responders in their communities in the event of a threat to the homeland.
Patriotic Education	Lessons provided on putting one's country before oneself; "Ask not what your country can do for you, but what you can do for your country"; e pluribus unum ("out of many, one"); service in a democratic republic.

NATIONAL SERVICE

Following basic training, national service is mandatory for a minimum of ten days per year for five years. However, maximum flexibility is the goal, and participants could choose to join programs that are already in place, such as the Peace Corps, AmeriCorps, Teach for America, military service, and others. For service in certain long-term commitment programs—the Peace Corps or Teach for America, for example—one full year of service would satisfy the national service requirement. Of course, military service would fulfill the national service requirement as well. The national service component can be deferred until after college for any program that requires such educational prerequisites.

The following are some of the options participants might choose from:

Option I	Begin national service immediately after basic training and education within an existing service program, such as AmeriCorps.
Option II	Begin by choosing from a database of duties for 5 years, 10 days per year. These may include guard duties at government buildings, work at veterans' centers, hospitals, etc.
Option III	Defer service until after college for service options that require further education.
Option IV	Volunteer/enlist for military service immediately following basic training or after college.

Through such a national service program, we will have—at last—a mechanism for cultivating a "unifying civic virtue" in the entire population of our future generations.

With a stronger focus on American values in the home and implemented patriotic school curricula, which we'll discuss in the next chapter, our young adults would enter the National Service Corps already possessing these essential American values. The national service program would introduce or reinforce the nation's first principles and founding values and the principles of gratitude, personal responsibility, and sacrifice, which serve as the driving mechanism to perpetuate these values. For at least some time in their life, all Americans will have had the experience of knowing what it means to sacrifice and take responsibility for themselves as well as for their fellow service men and women. They will have experienced "common cause" with those who one day may choose to serve in the military, and so will have forged a genuine connection with those who have resolved to give that last full measure of devotion to their nation. And our nation will be rejuvenated with a population of vibrant, strong, and disciplined young people who are prepared for the challenges that lie ahead.

When the relationship between citizen and citizen, and citizen and country, begins in charity, the force of gratitude in our society will pervade everything. This is not a fantasy of perfection. In the same way that we have managed to create an American sociology based upon liberty and an American commerce based upon personal responsibility, we must continue to develop an American culture based upon sacrifice and gratitude. The surest sign that this is once again America will be when we see future generations and immigrants shunning an attitude of entitlement and devoting at least some part of their lives in service to their communities and country, exhibiting gratitude for what they have received as citizens, and asking not what this country can do for them, but what they can do for America.

This spirit of gratitude, personal responsibility, and sacrifice is in the very fabric and force of what it means to be an American. It is only through this common framework of values that we will be able to build, maintain, and advance the last great hope for humanity—the United States of America.

11

RAISING THE NEXT GREAT(FUL) GENERATION

Bear in mind that the wonderful things you learn in your schools are the work of many generations. All this is put in your hands as your inheritance in order that you may receive it, honor it, add to it, and one day faithfully hand it on to your children.

—ALBERT EINSTEIN

The most logical, powerful, and sustaining solution to restoring our great nation lies with our children. It is our children who must embrace and embody our founding values.

Why children? Because of their youth, lack of cynicism, and capacity for deep adaptation, they have a long-term transformative capacity that adults generally do not possess. For any transformation to take hold in our country, it must begin with our children, as they will grow to be the future leaders. The attitudes and values they adopt, for better or worse, will be reflected in the direction they take this nation.

In *Good to Great* (HarperBusiness, 2001), Jim Collins reveals a simple "yawning truth": companies that have gone from good to great had a set of fixed principles, and their leaders focused on establishing more principles and promoting the growth of those principles. This ethic was passed seamlessly from leader to successor. Refocusing on our children means we all discover the possibility and necessity of leadership (we all become framers and founders) and our children become true, worthy, prepared successors. We will all move off stage someday, and so our children are successors in fact. But when we pass on our principles and values, we make them successors in substance.

This focus on our children would also have a positive effect on every adult, company, and government agency. The entire social, corporate, and political superstructure of this country would gain a new perspective that would reenergize our country in a hopeful direction toward our nation's core values. And that is an absolute necessity, considering why we are where we are.

If you are inspired by our founding values, believe in the transformative power of children, and believe that a focus on our children will have multi-level, unforeseeable positive effects, then you will likely agree that Americans need a principle, a program, a mechanism to achieve those effects. I believe such a program or mechanism should have three critical components:

- Parenting—Train children in our founding values.
- School curricula—Teach our founding values.
- National service—Practice our founding values.

Our reestablishment of American values and recommitment to passing down the American inheritance we have all been given must simultaneously begin with the initiation of a twofold commitment to a purposeful, patriotic model of parenting and educating, and to the commencement of a plan for national service we just discussed. This three-pronged approach will ensure that every child and every new adult will adopt the primary principles of gratitude, personal responsibility, and sacrifice.

THE PARENTS' ROLE

It is certainly a paradox that parents who worked so hard and sacrificed so much could come to believe that the more they gave their children, the greater the sense of satisfaction and feeling of success they would have and the "better" their children would be or become.

We want our children to have what we did not. It's understandable. It is a reflection of our generous spirit, which has not only motivated parents but also served as a measurement of the success of a family from one generation to the next. At one level, people who struggled wanted to ensure that their children did not know such struggles. It was as much for their children as it was for their own sense of personal accomplishment.

But more often than not, this sentiment leads to a sense of entitlement. Wanting our children to "have it better than we did" may assure that they do not.

Why? Because such thinking is rarely focused on wanting our children to lead a more principled life than we did. Instead, it contributes to the Paradox of Prosperity by reducing our children's advancement to purely material measures. And we fail to reinforce the values that are more likely to guarantee our children actually have it better than we did.

Parents generally don't want their children to ignore or avoid sacrifices or to lack proper gratitude for all the gifts they receive. But in simply wanting to provide a better life for their children, they are often unaware of the destructive, unintended consequences—both to their children and, by extension and extrapolation, to the nation—that come from such indulgences.

What, then, should parents do? The Bible offers this concrete advice: "Train a child in the way he should go, and when he is old he shall not depart from it" (Proverbs 22:6). The evocative power of that principle lies first in the assumption that whoever "trains" the child knows "the way he should go." It also implies there is an irrepressible memory in children, and if we are not training them in one way, they are learning another. Whatever that other way is, for some time now in our country it has certainly not been the personal responsibility, sacrifice, and gratitude, together with individualism, that are central to being an American.

This is a difficult and serious challenge. Every parent I talk with says that parents are spoiling their children, and all agree that it is ruining otherwise good children. Yet few parents look at themselves when agreeing to these statements. J. C. Ryle, a minister in the late nineteenth century, addressed the question of how the mistake of allowing our desire for our children's success, our attempts to shield them from our own struggles, and our inability to see what we are doing as we are doing it undermines the values that would actually give children the right attitude for success.

Everyone [should] ask himself the question, "In the matter of training children, am I doing what I am supposed to do?" . . . This is notably a point in
which [people] can see the faults of their neighbors more clearly than their
own . . . They will have the eyesight of an eagle in detecting mistakes everywhere else, and yet be blind as bats to the fatal errors which are daily going on
in their own homes. They will be wise about their brother's house, but foolish
about their own flesh and blood.[59]

As concerned, overworked, and anxious as parents are, their first focus
must be the situation in their homes, beginning with a total transformation in
thinking about child rearing.

- Parents must move past the need to defend their own acts and
  omissions, which may have contributed to the attitude of entitlement children exhibit so comprehensively across every community
  in our country.
- Parents must understand that we will live in the world our children
  will create from the perspective they gain from our guidance and
  instruction.
- Parents must come to a realization that the values required in a
  healthy parent-child relationship are exactly the ones required for
  mature citizenship. The very things that make a child responsible,
  respectful, and grateful are the same things that make a child a great
  citizen—a true American who will help perpetuate a great America.

Parents are faced with an unprecedented barrage of challenges to their
authority and direct influence on their children. Our very culture is the cul-
prit; ours is a culture in which people think primarily *of* themselves while,
ironically, thinking less *for* themselves. The world is becoming increasingly
narcissistic. The advent of social networking gives everyone an opportunity to
pretend celebrity without the commitment to earning recognition through
talent and effort. Sadly, this reinforces poor habits of judgment and responsibility because it undermines perspective.

Yet almost no parent has been trained specifically to raise children, and
certainly parents have not been trained to raise children who understand
what it means to be an American—in the way that our grandparents (the

Greatest Generation) understood it—to embrace and embody America's first principles and founding values. Even where parents themselves may have been exposed to the grace of deference and rules of good parenting, they may not have absorbed the practices of their own good parents sufficiently to put those practices into operation. This is no different from an athlete who is well coached, who thrives from the excellence of that coaching, but cannot explain what the methods were that brought him to the point of greatness.

Parents must understand and then cultivate in their children, from the earliest stages of life, a system of respect and honor. If children do not develop a sense of respect, honor, and gratitude for the sacrifices that are made by their parents, who are in their immediate sphere of influence, how will they ever be able to develop a sense of respect, honor, and gratitude for sacrifices made by those who are far removed—whether by time or by distance—from their immediate sphere?

So let's explore how parents can instill respect and honor, responsibility and gratitude in their children.

TEACHING GRATITUDE AND SACRIFICE

A child comes into this world and receives the care of parents. These parents make innumerable sacrifices long before the child is born and long after. These sacrifices demand a thousand alterations of existing plans, objectives, and opportunities, often just for the sake of the child. Most parents undertake these sacrifices willingly and almost always without realizing the hidden costs to themselves. The arrival of the child is the beginning of a lifelong routine of sacrifices, without any assurance that those sacrifices will be acknowledged, understood, or appreciated.

In fact, it is a primary duty of parents to themselves recognize, understand, and appreciate those sacrifices. And it is a primary duty of a child—as early in life as possible—to learn about these sacrifices, to recognize and understand them, and to develop an enduring gratitude for them.

To appreciate the sacrifices parents make, beyond merely recognizing or understanding them, means that you have insight into what it means to be an "absolute beneficiary." Children can never know, imagine, or repay the sacrifices of which they are beneficiaries. To appreciate them despite this is the only valuable form of gratitude.

This gratitude—the appreciation that the totality of the sacrifices made is unknowable—gives birth to an understanding and motivation that the only way to show gratitude is to make sacrifices of our own, and to vigilantly ensure that this appreciation for parents' sacrifices is reflected each day in the way we conduct ourselves and the choices we make.

It is summed up this way in *The Hidden Costs—What Children Owe to Parents*:

> Children are born in arrears. As parents we dream of their maturity, independence, and success. A child must come as soon as possible to know this dream, and it is their duty, to note all that has been sacrificed to make that dream come true; because each of us, when we reflect our parents' hopes in having been respectful, thoughtful children and grow into mature, resourceful, and successful adults, we are nothing short of dreams fulfilled. And that is the only means we have to repay—in a manner of speaking—all the sacrifices undertaken for us. It all begins with our recognition of those sacrifices, at the earliest possible stage of life. This leads to gratitude or a burning impulse to satisfy and honor parents, motivated by those numberless sacrifices. And this leads us to see the value of sacrifices as well. This is the cycle of life.[60]

To coin a variation on President Kennedy's famous aphorism quoted earlier, children should be taught this motto: "Ask not what your parents can do for you but what you can do for your parents." This is the minimum expression of recognizing that one is the beneficiary of something that cannot be repaid. It is startling to me that this structure is not more prominent in a nation that requires sacrifices for the maintenance of its values.

But for these values to take hold, the sacrifices made must become a form of instruction. We should share the hardships we have endured with our children. Parents must find as many means as possible, as early in children's lives as possible, to instill recognition of the sacrifices on which the children themselves survive and thrive. More than that, we should give them responsibilities to help them understand why we must make sacrifices to earn rewards. They should understand what it takes to make something of oneself, apart from the head start they may have been given by a parent who has endured hardships.

Teaching children from this perspective is goal-oriented parenting, and it is the only approach that doesn't leave it to the external forces of the world—friends, school, and society—to shape the character of our children.

WHY THE PARENTS' ROLE IS CRITICAL

Neuroscience has shown that in the first three years of life, children are more susceptible to learning than in any other period of their lives. And it's not just absorption of information. The very construction of the child's brain is being mapped and affected.

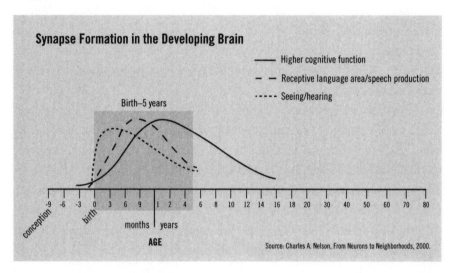

Source: Charles A. Nelson, From Neurons to Neighborhoods, 2000.

What makes the brain grow is the affection, instruction, and exposure parents provide, supported by an environment that delivers additional stimuli.

This means that our best opportunity to influence the way America develops is for parents to rear their children with the sense of individualism and personal responsibility, powered by sacrifice and gratitude, from day one. This leads not merely to respectful, resourceful children but also to loyal and active citizenship.

In the 1930s, H. M. Skeels conducted a study in which forty mentally retarded children were taken out of an orphanage and given to forty mothers. After four years, the forty orphans were found to have IQs fifty points higher than those who were left in the orphanage. Amazingly, the forty mothers themselves all suffered from mental retardation and were in a separate institution.

Nurturing is crucial to the development of the intellectual capacity of children, even if provided by a parent who may score lower on IQ or cognition tests than his or her children do.

Nineteen years ago, Katarina Bjurstedt, now a midwifery administrator in the United Kingdom, wrote an essay on the "synaptic process of brain formation" in children. Her conclusion was, "Culture becomes biology." We have often taken for granted the general idea that children are both influenced and impacted by their environment. The renowned Austrian psychologist Dr. Sigmund Freud became popular in the twentieth century because of a host of ideas—not all of them palatable—about early child development. Freud, who was himself a physician trained in pediatrics and neurology, came to believe that acknowledging and monitoring "drives" in children should be the focus of early child development.

For nearly half a century, Freud's ideas about child development dominated the literature in the child development field. In recent decades, however, a new approach was initiated by neurobiologists who thought we knew too little about the impact we ourselves have, or the impact both the environment we create and the historical and social environment in which we are locked have, on a child's brain development. The essence of what has been discovered over this period is simply breathtaking and applies to every child, regardless of gender, race, or social circumstances.

- Early experiences do not merely influence the mind of the child; they actually construct the brain.
- The critical timeline for this brain construction is birth to seven years old; within that time frame, birth to three years of age is particularly crucial.
- The early experience or "stimuli" continue to have an effect on the child's choices well into adulthood.

What these findings suggest and reinforce is that the parental role in early child development is paramount. They show that any change we wish to see in society and the changes we do see (for better or worse) are largely in the hands of parents to cultivate or to impart by the contents of parental influence or even neglect.

Here is how this point was addressed in a Harvard University study on the subject. In a paper titled "The Timing and Quality of Early Experiences Combine to Shape Brain Architecture," the research team wrote in the introduction:

The foundations of brain architecture are established early in life through a continuous series of dynamic interactions in which environmental conditions and personal experiences have a significant impact on how genetic predispositions are expressed. Because specific experiences affect specific brain circuits during specific developmental stages—referred to as sensitive periods—it is vitally important to take advantage of these early opportunities in the developmental building process . . . The quality of a child's early environment and the availability of appropriate experiences at the right stages of development are crucial in determining the strength or weakness of the brain's architecture, which, in turn, determines how well he or she will be able to think and to regulate emotions.[61]

A study presented by Charles A. Nelson in *From Neurons to Neighborhoods* (National Academies Press, 2000), showed that the "peak time" for brain development is the ninth month through the third year. Beyond the peak, there is continued brain development, but by the fifteenth year, the brain has an established synaptic pattern that affects how the young adult assesses situations, makes decisions and judgments, and, consequently, behaves. Of course, parents who are respected can still influence for good or ill, but any alteration in perspective must compete with a fully operational worldview.

This research offers scientific support for the idea that if we "train a child in the way it should go, when it is old it will not depart from our instruction." Why? Because the earliest instruction is "webbed" into the physical structure of the brain so that when in conflict or under pressure, the child is fortified in its deeply rooted and literally embedded knowledge of what is right to do in the circumstances. It is critical that we ensure the deep presence of such early parental instruction so that the child has something to capture or something from which he or she refuses to depart from in later years. We should undertake goal-directed parenting to take advantage of these key facts:

- Even at the earliest stages of life, children are learning, categorizing, positioning.

- There is no such thing as "idle minds." Whether we can determine it or not, they are observing and learning.
- In the process of our interactions with children, we should not lose the opportunities for imparting values.

And so, behavior that embodies the founding values should be modeled and taught at the earliest possible stage.

RESPECT AND HONOR: THE SIGNS OF A CHILD RAISED WITH VALUES

Let me share a family story to emphasize these principles and values in operation.

It was 1949. My father was seventeen years old and a junior in high school. He had established himself as one of the top athletes in the state of New Jersey. To say he was popular would be an understatement. And while he was always very respectful, he was also a bit cocky.

His team had just won the league championship and they were feeling on top of the world. The next day, after going to mandatory mass in the morning, he and other members of the team decided they would play hooky and enjoy what they believed was a well-deserved "self-designated holiday." Instead of going to class, they went to the local pool hall. Around lunchtime, a classmate came to the pool hall and told them the school administration was looking for them. They hadn't mentioned my father's name, so the classmate didn't think the school knew my father was part of the group that had cut school. Everyone except my father returned to school.

The next day, my father went to school as if nothing had happened. About mid-morning, one of the school secretaries appeared at his classroom door and said the principal wanted to see him in her office. As he walked into the principal's office, he saw four people just standing there, waiting: the principal (Sister Marie), his father, his mother, and Monsignor Brestol, the highest-ranking person in the parish.

I should add at this point that my father's father had an intimidating presence. He had only to look at you with "that look" and your stomach would churn and you'd get a bit weak in the knees. He was a very generous man and loved his family like few I have known, but he was tough. He grew up as the youngest of five children in an immigrant family in the Bronx and then in

Lodi, New Jersey. These were places where you often had to fight every day for your survival. He had to drop out of school after the eighth grade to help support his family.

My grandfather never once hit my father; he didn't have to. His rules, or "code," were very simple—respect and honor. He believed that without respect, you have nothing. If you have respect then all the other important attributes will be present automatically. If you truly respect and honor your parents it will never occur to you to lie to them or to disobey them without remorse. If you respect yourself you will never think about acting out at school or doing something you know would likely tarnish your name or reputation.

My grandmother was a tiny woman, but she had a heart the size of Florence Nightingale's and the courage of Joan of Arc. I think "kind" would be the best way to describe her. She had a way of making everyone and anyone she met feel welcome and at home. Even strangers were always welcome into her home for a plate of macaroni. "Mangiare" ("eat") she would urge everyone, confident there was nothing a good plate of macaroni couldn't fix. In fact, she believed the dinner table formed the core and foundation for the family. It was during meals that she and my grandfather had my father's undivided attention and thus the opportunity to instill their values. While it may sound cliché, it is nonetheless accurate to say that I never heard anyone say a bad word about my grandmother. My grandfather was the king of the house, but my grandmother was truly the glue that held the family together.

This is what my father faced as he walked into the principal's office. He knew that the four adults all knew what he had done. He expected a reprimand from the principal and "that look" and a loud scolding from his father. So my father decided he would try to explain. As the first syllable left his mouth, my grandmother held up her hand as if to say, "not a word." My father immediately fell silent. My grandmother, all four-foot-eleven of her, walked up to my nearly six-foot father and *whack*—she slapped him across the face so hard he felt his teeth rattle. "Is this how you respect me? Is this how you show respect for your family and your name?" she asked.

When my grandmother slapped my father, I believe what he felt was the pain she felt. She had worked all her life. She was honest and diligent. She and my grandfather had made a life for their family, never complaining, always willing to listen to and help with other people's troubles, even when those troubles were less than their own. My grandfather was grateful for America, the life it afforded him and the opportunities it provided for a son like my father. My father saw all of this, and saw, too, that they could not understand how their son could get it in his head to disrespect everything they believed in.

My father simply stood there. Not a flinch, not a word. He knew he was wrong, and more importantly, he knew his conduct was an act of disrespect, that it was like a knife in my grandmother's heart. What he had done was a direct assault on everything she stood for and everything she raised him to stand for.

Today, my father's behavior might be seen as "no big deal." Today, the child in my father's position would be tempted to think that somehow his athletic achievement was some sort of benefit to his parents, as if they were privileged to have him as their child. Many parents today, I fear, would dismiss this behavior as "acting out" or "being young and foolish" and would fail to detect the sense of entitlement inherent in it. More tragically, they would fail to see they had allowed this behavior to fester as a result of their failure to discipline, never making it clear to the child that his limited perspective doesn't offer an accurate account of the magnitude of the wrong committed.

And any children who have been allowed to develop the notion that they can define the degree to which they will accept responsibility in such a situation can never respect or honor their parents or anyone else. Any parent who allows a child to determine the level and meaning of this or any such behavior, or who hides behind the vacuous idea of "going through phases" or "acting out" can never hope to enjoy the level of respect, admiration, and adoration my father showed toward my grandmother that day.

The next day, my father ran into Monsignor Brestol, who pulled him aside and said he had always admired my father as an athlete and as a young man, but after what he had observed of him the day before, he had a whole new level of admiration. My father was confused. Monsignor Brestol explained: He had watched my grandmother slap him, and my father didn't react, didn't complain, didn't answer back. He just stood like a man and took it. It is a rare thing to see such respect, such character, the monsignor said. From that moment on, my father and Monsignor Brestol forged what would become a lifelong friendship.

What I find so profound yet so simple about this story is that my father's reaction in standing and accepting this punishment and humiliation demonstrated the exact values he had failed to demonstrate the day before, causing him to face such punishment. In that very moment, I must imagine, he demonstrated to my grandmother and grandfather that they had raised him as they had hoped and had, in fact, instilled in him this most fundamental value.

My grandparents made a life for my father; they demanded of him and provided examples of responsibility, sacrifice, and gratitude. For these—and a thousand additional sacrifices—my father was grateful.

The true test of gratitude, shown as respect, is how one behaves in difficult situations, when there is no reason to be respectful other than that you are actually interested in being respectful. Gratitude is not a word or phrase. Gratitude is a set of actions motivated by an irresistible need to compensate for a sacrifice, and it aims to assure the person who made the sacrifice that it is appreciated. If the person who made the sacrifice seems unsure of our appreciation the fault must lie with us, because the person who made the sacrifice has already given something priceless. So it is unlikely that that same person will fail to acknowledge an action confirming our appreciation.

The difficulty we face today is that parents do not demand and children do not show the sort of respect my father displayed. So many children have become the tail that wags the dog; parents seem helpless, imprisoned by the erroneous idea that being supportive and being liked are more important than being respected for the priceless sacrifices they have made.

When the most basic relationship between parents and children is weakened and diseased, all relationships are weakened and diseased. It is impossible for there to be dysfunction in the first and excellence in the others.

Parenting carries within it certain aspects of respect, honor, and courtesy that are not just between a parent and a child. These virtues must be transmitted from one generation to the next. They are the right values for citizenship. And when a nation produces citizens who possess these attributes, that nation can once again rise to greatness.

THE ROLE OF EDUCATORS

While it is the duty of parents to teach the values that will help their children grow into mature, responsible adults and strong American citizens, we must support those efforts in our schools. And, given that many children grow up without encountering these values and lack the discipline or the perspectives these values naturally support, there must be a mechanism to impress their importance upon their minds.

Our educational system seems the most logical means for imparting our founding values to our children. Yet as we previously discussed, our schools do a poor job teaching the critical information of citizenship. Obviously, some changes must be made if we are going to rely on them to do more. Let's first explore the very practical reasons why we should invest in better and earlier education for our youth.

THE CASE FOR EARLY CHILDHOOD EDUCATION

The Federal Reserve Board has been at the forefront of discussions concerning economic priorities. As part of that focus, they do much research on how economies grow and what factors contribute to that growth. One factor they and other economists have homed in on is the quality of the workforce. Two economists with the Minneapolis Federal Reserve Bank have released a report addressing the issue of early childhood education and how it impacts our future workforce. "Investments in human capital prior to kindergarten . . . can make a substantial impact on the success of children's futures as students, workers and citizens in democratic society. [It] is the most efficient means to boost the productivity of the workforce 15 to 20 years down the road . . . [It] yields a much higher return than most government-funded economic development initiatives."[62]

James Heckman, a Nobel Prize–winning economist, maps the effect of early childhood education this way: "Enriching the early years will promote the productivity of schools by giving teachers better quality students. Improving the schools will in turn improve the quality of the workforce."[63]

The question is how do we get from here to there?

I believe investments in early childhood development (ECD) programs are a starting point. While I have been critical of unnecessary government spending, particularly in the form of entitlements, what I'm proposing here is an investment of tax dollars that could keep future generations in school, off welfare, and contributing to the economic strength of our country. And the investment to create programs for low-income children (children from families that can afford such programs are already experiencing the benefits) would be minimal compared to other expenditures.

Why?

First, it's effective. Research shows that, in almost every case, the returns in performance for participating children have been remarkable, as the Minneapolis Fed explained above. While the studies concentrated on poor families with at-risk children, a thorough ongoing focus on our entire constituency of pre-K through third graders would produce unprecedented impacts in our future financial security as a nation.

Second, it's profitable. In almost every case where studies have been undertaken, it has been shown that investment in ECD not only advanced the education and opportunities for the children who participated but also provided a cost-benefit ratio that exceeds 3:1, or three dollars for every one dollar invested. Incredibly, the most notable studies—the Perry Pre-School Program, the Abecedarian Project, the Chicago Child-Parent Centers project, and the Elmira Pre-Natal/Early Infancy Project—all demonstrated annualized rates of return ranging from 7 to 18 percent.

Third, programs and plans are already in place that would make this idea immediately implementable. Of course, there would be a substantial initial cost, but we would recoup that cost in a host of ways. The economists at the Minneapolis Fed estimated that in Minneapolis, an initial outlay of $1.5 billion, invested to earn 6 to 7 percent annually would cover the costs of scholarships for all young children living below the poverty level, program administration, teacher training, and other costs.

So here we have a plan that is needed to advance this nation and its values, is profitable, and is doable. In recent years, the federal government has earmarked $700 billion for bank bailouts, spent $50 billion to bail out General Motors, and added trillions (and counting) to the budget deficit and national debt for a variety of initiatives, none of which have proven as effective as promised.

What would happen if, as the Minneapolis Fed advises, we applied an appropriate portion of those funds to early childhood education for low-income and at-risk children who would otherwise likely become dropouts and a cost to society?

In the face of the variety of challenges facing our country, and given the findings that a host of studies have revealed about the potential impact on our social and economic life, investing in early childhood development for our underprivileged and at-risk children is not only our duty as a nation but also a profitable strategy.

TEACHING PATRIOTISM AND FOUNDING VALUES

The political partisanship in America has become so vitriolic we can hardly agree on the bare facts of our history, much less how we should teach them. One term in particular has been misused so much it has become a signal of and substitute for propaganda. That term is "patriotism."

In a working paper published by the Center for Information and Research on Civic Learning and Engagement, William Damon wrote the following: "Patriotism is the most politically incorrect word in education today. Teachers too often confuse a patriotic love of country with . . . militaristic chauvinism. They do not seem to realize that it was . . . patriotic resistance . . . that saved the world from tyranny in the past century and is the best hope of doing so in the future."[64]

The word "patriotism" has become a loaded word in this divisive period of partisan American politics. Damon recognized a fear associated with the word, a fear of treating the shortfalls of the nation lightly, without intellectual honesty, in favor of whitewashed, vacuous cheerleading that fails to acknowledge the nation's fall away from its values.

If you believe American values are malleable or America's values were empty from day one—or became empty on the backs of slavery, Native American slaughter, the mistreatment of women, or any of a hundred other deeds that undermine those values—then patriotism in education is likely a problem for you.

If, however, you believe America's values are timeless; if you believe the history of this nation has been a steady trek on the path to a more perfect union, even though we may not have always lived up to our values; if you believe the values are perfect and it's the people who have at times been less than what the values promised; if you believe we must find our way back toward our original values—then patriotic education is merely a tactic to achieve the ends of guiding our young people toward our most cherished principles.

Are there opportunities for abuse? Yes, of course. It is an understandable concern that if we teach patriotism in our schools and as part of a national service program such education could dissolve into propaganda and an opportunity for ideologues to advance their specific agendas. It would be intellectually dishonest to disregard this risk. However, it is typical of something that is necessary but also difficult. And there are sufficient opportunities for abuse in our current educational system that can lead our young people away from our nation's founding values. In the absence of teaching our values, an even greater variety of ideologues will seek to shape our children's minds. If we are to err it seems only logical to err on the side of our founding values.

SCOUTS: HOW PATRIOTISM IS ALREADY BEING TAUGHT

While it is crucial for us to do a better job all around of teaching our youth what it means to be American, could it be that on the question of patriotic education we are arguing about something that has already been done and is currently being done?

For most Americans there are few if any opportunities to express and act upon an oath or some other sort of commitment to this country. That must change. But one of the most notable, best known, oft repeated, but least acknowledged examples we have of such an oath in America are the Boy Scout and Girl Scout oaths.

It turns out that over the past hundred years, the potentially controversial "patriotic education" we advocate has been taught to nearly 100 million Boy Scouts and to more than 50 million Girl Scouts.

A close examination of what we have been recommending and what the Scouts have been teaching shows a striking resemblance to the character development that should necessarily grow from our founding values. Both the Boy Scouts and the Girl Scouts of America aim to train their young charges in responsible citizenship and character development. Through a series of tests and outdoor challenges, they teach self-reliance, often in partnership with community organizations.

The values of the Scouts are very much in need, particularly in a society overrun by an attitude and culture of entitlement and complaint. Those values are trustworthiness, respect, character, good citizenship, volunteerism, and self-governance.

THE CURRICULUM OF PATRIOTISM

The standard established by the founding values of America produced a form of liberty and a degree of prosperity of which our children are inheritors. They must be able, therefore, to recognize, understand, and advocate for those values and the benefits they hold in store. They must learn them at the earliest possible stage of life and then have those values reinforced by a school curriculum.

Establishing such a curriculum, however, would be fraught with known and unknown challenges, such as the following:

- A lack of understanding and will at the political level
- Little connection among the promise of *e pluribus unum*, our founding values, and our modern social and political discourse
- Apathy toward the meaning of the American ethic, with even those who are patriotic insisting on and perpetuating attitudes that are inconsistent with the values themselves
- A large body of our citizenry rejecting the idea of American greatness or viewing American values as principles the nation has breached time and again
- Disagreements over whether teaching the founding values is propagandistic

Yet the most unbelievable and ironic challenge is that the teaching of the basic documents of America's founding, with an emphasis on our trek toward a more perfect union, may prove too controversial.

Read, for instance, the following text, which appears on the inside cover of a published version of the U.S. Constitution and the Declaration of Independence (Wilder Publications/A&D Publishing, 2007):

This book is a product of its time and does not reflect the same values as it would if it were written today. Parents might wish to discuss with their children how views on race, gender, sexuality, ethnicity, and interpersonal relations have changed since this book was written before allowing them to read this classic work.

We make no effort here to scandalize Wilder Publications. They may have felt this disclaimer was an act of fairness. But this is misguided. It is hard to imagine a French publication of the Declaration of the Rights of Man and Citizens—its founding document—in which the publisher apologizes for possible implications of injustice in the text. It is not the values that have changed. The application of those values, however, and the concepts of what is just certainly have, all in our effort to form a more perfect union. There is no denying that America had and has much to answer for. However, our history is the history—more than that of any other nation—of providing such answers.

And providing those answers should be the focus of any patriotic education.

If we are to restore America to its greatness, our schools must play an important role and incorporate into their curricula a capstone course that is designed to

- Teach the history of our constant march toward a more perfect union;
- Teach our first principles and founding values (including our founding documents and their significance) and how those values not only created a land of opportunity that attracted immigrants from across the globe but also created the wealthiest and most generous nation in the history of mankind; and
- Instill a sense of patriotism in our young people.

This is what American children, naturalized children, and the children of foreigners at school in America should learn as essential about America, and essential about being an American. It is what all immigrants should pledge faith and fealty to, so that they understand that if they are met with an injustice inconsistent with our values, there is no need to attempt to destroy this nation. Unlike so many other nations, our system provides in its basic structure and values a means to correct injustices and provide the maximum human liberty possible under the rule of law.

We recognize the fear of teaching patriotic curricula in our schools. We recognize the opportunity for ideologues to attempt to advance their agendas and to deny the sufferings caused by our fall away from what our values promised. However, our founding values require criticism of American policies, social practices, and political decisions as essential to our pathway toward a more perfect union.

Parents live with this eternal anxiety: Once they have taught children the way they should go, they worry that those children will depart from it. And if they depart, they may not return to those teachings. Teachers know this feeling too: On the first day of class, they feel the anxiety of the future. They know almost instantly which students are ready for the world, which think they are ready and are not, and which—with a little care, but with so little time—may be turned around or opened up or focused upon their potential successfully.

I hope the children of this nation gain maturity and those with maturity gain skill. And then, when we hang everything upon them, when they enter a world that training could never forecast accurately, I hope their training "bubbles up" and disciplines them toward the ends to which their efforts are applied.

These hopes are not flawed. If we train them in the way they should go, they will not depart from it. It's a scientific fact. But it is our responsibility to train them. And we must start right now.

12

THE POWER OF ONE

As we express our gratitude, we must never forget that the highest appreciation is not to utter words, but to live by them.

—John Fitzgerald Kennedy

If not you, who? If not now, when?

"What difference can I make? I'm just one person." This protest is often heard from adults and children alike. It seems we live in a world where individuals no longer believe they matter or can make a difference. People feel helpless to influence the course of events that will shape their future and that of their children.

It's easy to understand how one could come to feel small and insignificant. The massiveness of the political and social spectacles of life we see all around us through a twenty-four-hour global news cycle is nothing short of mind numbing: trillions of dollars being spent like monopoly money; armed nations rattling their sabers and threatening the safety and very existence of their neighbors; soldiers patrolling the globe in search of a web of fanatics; and advancements in technology—both positive and negative—happening in the time it takes us to make a cup of coffee.

With this feeling of helplessness, how do we revive a nation and restore its spirit and its values? It is my belief that it begins with the individual. Edmund

Burke is often credited with saying, "All that is necessary for the triumph of evil is that good men do nothing."[65] Conveying this sentiment more fully, he wrote:

> It is not enough in a situation of trust in the commonwealth, that a man means well to his country; it is not enough that in his single person he never did an evil act, but always voted according to his conscience, and even harangued against every design which he apprehended to be prejudicial to the interests of his country. This innoxious and ineffectual character . . . falls miserably short of the mark of public duty. That duty demands and requires, that what is right should not only be made known, but made prevalent; that what is evil should not only be detected, but defeated.[66]

The *power of one* is the recognition that one person can make a difference. To be sure, the power of one is not about the search for that one person, like Neo in *The Matrix*, who will save America or the world. Rather, it is the recognition of the cumulative and compounding impact and power of individuals who each take responsibility for themselves and their actions. It's the impact and power of individuals standing up for what they believe and participating in the process of restoring America to its greatness. It's about individuals, starting with you, making a commitment to embrace the values and principles upon which this country was founded and ensuring that those values are reflected in your everyday life.

President George H. W. Bush made this point in his 1989 inaugural speech: "I have spoken of a thousand points of light, of all the community organizations that are spread like stars throughout the Nation, doing good. We will work hand in hand, encouraging, sometimes leading, sometimes being led, rewarding . . . The old ideas are new again because they are not old, they are timeless: duty, sacrifice, commitment, and a patriotism that finds its expression in taking part and pitching in."

We can see this type of cumulative and compounding individualism throughout our nation's short history, beginning with the Founding Fathers. Jefferson, Adams, Madison, Franklin, and Washington, to name a few, each played an instrumental role in the independence and framing of America. Each different, each individual. But together they created a movement that changed the world and the course of history.

Beneath the constellation of our founding values came those who continued to build and make the republic. Some names are forgotten to history, others—Abraham Lincoln, Frederick Douglass, Dr. Martin Luther King Jr.—embody the spirit of those forgotten. By their individual actions, they reinvented the notion and the hope that the republic the founders envisioned would not only come into being but would also "live out the true meaning of its creed."

This idea of the *power of one* is so powerful that we see it lauded in our media (although the stories are often buried beneath the trials and tribulations of the world) and furthered in our literature, movies, and other forms of expression. One of the most famous examples of this is the idea of "paying it forward." Catherine Ryan Hyde brought this concept to mainstream awareness with her book *Pay it Forward*, in which a twelve-year-old boy's social studies class is given an assignment to come up with an idea that would make the world a better place. The young boy conceives of the idea of "paying it forward," imagining that if he were to perform three good deeds for other people and, as repayment for receiving those good deeds, each of those people would perform three good deeds for others, and so on, an exponential wave of kindness and goodness could take hold and sweep across the land and literally make the world a better place.

This is the *power of one*. The recognition that each of us has within us, regardless of profession, income, or background, the ability to do something—no matter how small or seemingly insignificant in the big scheme of the world—that makes a difference in someone else's life. A simple unexpected smile or a helping hand in a moment of despair may be all someone needs to make his or her life more meaningful.

To many, this idea may seem innocent, naive, even foolhardy. But consider that the very idea of America, at the time of its conception, was itself unprecedented. The idea in Hyde's book took hold in real life, beginning with the Pay it Forward Foundation, which brings the idea of paying it forward to students and teachers around the world. The idea became even more mainstream in 2006 when Oprah adopted the idea and gave three hundred members of her audience each one thousand dollars, with the challenge of paying it forward by using the funds to perform acts of kindness toward others.

Paying it forward is the embodiment of the fundamental ideas of sacrifice and gratitude. Each person, grateful for the sacrifices that have been made for him or her, demonstrates gratitude by a further act of sacrifice that clearly demonstrates and leaves no doubt as to the gratitude felt.

Personal responsibility is central to the idea of paying it forward because a sacrifice that is a willing sacrifice, conceived by the individual without pressure from any outside source, is more moving and meaningful. And it is this that unleashes—pays forward—a thousand "points of light" of gratitude and additional sacrifice. We each must first recognize, understand, and appreciate the sacrifices that have been made for our benefit, must feel gratitude for those sacrifices, then in turn pay it forward (sacrifice for another).

In the structure of paying it forward, before we have something for which to be grateful, someone must make an initial sacrifice, not motivated or inspired by some previous act of sacrifice but by belief in values and a set of principles. The giving of a gift is an act of integrity, and we act from integrity when we are motivated not by a previous good deed but when we are blind to any outcome of our actions, driven instead by the principles and values we believe in. And so in giving that gift, we give to ourselves, to our communities, and to our country.

This, in essence, is what America means. The founders had no examples to follow. They moved on this great enterprise driven by principles they thought were permanent and values they believed to be eternal. And this is what it means to be an American—to be one who finds his worth in values and his guide to living in principles above traditions and the accidental habits of history.

History is rich with examples of those who acted with no other motivation than principles and values. One is reminded, for instance, of the movie *Freedom Writers*, the true story of Erin Gruwell (played by Hilary Swank), a young teacher who was assigned to a class of at-risk students at a recently integrated school in California. Overcoming many challenges both from within the classroom and from the school system itself, she helps guide this group of "unteachables" to learn tolerance, to respect each other, and to apply themselves in ways they never thought possible.

While reading *The Diary of Anne Frank*, the class learns that one of the women in the book, Miep Gies—who had helped hide Anne Frank and eight other Jews from the Germans during the Second World War—was then eighty-seven years old and living in Austria. After she accepts their invitation to meet with them at their school, the class raises the money and arranges for Miep Gies to fly to California.

During her visit, a student who was clearly inspired and moved by her courage and sacrifice for others, stands and tells her that while he had never had a hero before, she is his hero. Miep Gies responds, "Oh, no. No, no, no, young man, no. I am not a hero. No. I did what I had to do because it was the right thing to do. That is all."

One person, doing what was right, sacrificing for others. Not knowing what ripple effect it would have for future generations who would hear and read her story.

Then Miep Gies continues: "We are all ordinary people. But even an ordinary secretary, or a housewife, or a teenager can within their own small ways turn on a small light in a dark room."

By understanding and applying the *power of one* to the founding values of personal responsibility, sacrifice, and gratitude, we are perpetuating those values for future generations so that they may enjoy and perpetuate the greatness that is America.

Nations rise and fall. History is replete with the bleached bones of men and nations that thought they could follow two impossible paths: ignore the virtues of prudence and principles, and do so indefinitely. In our case, less than fifty years into the greatest economic expansion in human history, the celebratory mood is overcome with denial, indifference, and indulgence. And what was once unthinkable—perhaps foolishly—has become incandescent chatter across the entire world: America is in decline.

Why rescue America?

Because America is the last great hope for mankind and provides liberty, opportunity, and prosperity for more people than any other endeavor in human history. America is the beacon of hope for people around the world. If not America, then what?

If we are what this nation was established for us to become, then we must meet this great challenge of our lifetime. Let's turn on the light in our dark rooms, and let's not look to politicians or economists or pundits of the right or left to rescue our nation. Let's look to ourselves—American heirs—and ask:

"If not me, then who? If not now, then when?"

ENDNOTES

1. Thomas Jefferson in a letter to Thomas Mann Randolph, May 30,1790 (See also: Andrés Marroquín, ed., *Invisible Hand: The Wealth of Adam Smith*, and Robert L. Hetzel, *The Relevance of Adam Smith,* page 25).

2. Andrés Marroquín, ed., *Invisible Hand: The Wealth of Adam Smith* (University Press of the Pacific, 2002), 24-25.

3. Adam Smith, *An Inquiry into the Nature and Causes of the Wealth of Nations* (General Books LLC, 2010), part IV.5.82

4. Matthew 7:12, Matthew 22:39, Luke 6:31.

5. Aristotle, *The Nicomachean Ethics*, 1101a10.

6. Henry Louis Gates Jr., ed., and Donald Yacovone, ed., *Lincoln on Race and Slavery* (Princeton University Press), 343.

7. "Total Economy Database, Summary Statistics, 1995–2010," The Conference Board Total Economy Database, The Conference Board, September 2010; retrieved 9/20/2009.

8. "Doing Business in the United States (2006)," World Bank; retrieved 6/28/2007.

9. Luke 12:48.

10. Enrique R. Carrasco, "The Business Transactions of Migrants: Remittances," 2."

11. Julie Kim and Steven Woehrel, "Kosovo and U.S. Policy: Background to Independence," CRS Report for Congress, June 20, 2008, RL31053, Congressional Research Service, Library of Congress, Washington, D.C.

12. Helmut Schmidt, "I Believe in America," *The Atlantic Times*, July 2007: <http://www.atlantic-times.com/archive_detail.php?recordID=935>.

13. "Sinclair soothes a suffering U.S.," Bruce Garvey, Toronto Star, November 28, 1973, p. A1.

14. © 1973 Gordon Sinclair. Published by Star Quality Music (Socan), A division of UNIDISC MUSIC, INC. 578 Hymus Boulevard, Pointe-Claire, Quebec, Canada, H9R4T2

15. Alexis de Tocqueville, *Democracy in America*, Volume I – Chapter XIII

16. Edward Gibbon, *The History of the Decline and Fall of the Roman Empire*, Volume 1 (FQ Books, 2010), 529.

17. Own Devices: The Past and Future of Body Technology, Edward Tenner - Alfred A. Knopf. Also www.American Heritage.com, Invention & Technology Magazine 2008, "Hardheaded Logic" by Edward Tenner.

18. F. A. Hayek, *Individualism and Economic Order* (University of Chicago Press: 1996), 77.

19.   John Rawls, *A Theory of Justice* (Cambridge: Belknap Press, 1999), 137.

20.   Ibid., 11.

21.   David Von Drehle, "In the U.S., Crisis in the Statehouses," *Time Magazine*, June 17, 2010, http://www.time.com/time/nation/article/0,8599,1997284,00.html.

22.   Josh Boose, "Financial Problems Grow for New York State," www.wgrz.com, August 20, 2009, http://www.wgrz.com/news/local/story.aspx?storyid=69635&provider=gnews.

23.   Andrew Biggs, "Entitlement Apocalypse," *National Review Online*, March 30, 2010.

24.   Austan Goolsbee, "The Index of Missing Economic Indicators; The Unemployment Myth," *The New York Times*, November 30, 2003.

25.   Organization for Economic Cooperation and Development, "Income Distribution: Poverty" data available through the OECD.Stat Databas, http://stats.oecd.org/Index.aspx?QueryId=9909&QueryType=View; data published in "Growing Unequal? Income Distribution and Poverty in OECD Countries," www.oced.org, October 2008.

26.   The Legatum Institute, "The 2010 Prosperity Index," www.prosperity.com.

27.   Congressional Budget Office, "The Long-Term Budget Outlook (Summary)," June 2010, www.cbo.gov/doc.cfm?index=11579.

28.   Buttonwood, "Birth pains: A New Global System Is Coming into Existence," *The Economist*, May 14, 2009.

29.   John Lyman, "U.S. Military: Stretched Too Thin?" *Foreign Policy Digest*, February 1, 2009, http://www.foreignpolicydigest.org/2010/02/01/u-s-military-stretched-too-thin/.

30.   Chris Nelder, "China: The Vampire Squid of Commodities," *Business Insider Green Sheet*, November 23, 2009, www.businessinsider.com/china-the-vampire-squid-of-commodities-2009-11#ixzz0rQkH4kMz.

31.   Richard Behar, "Special Report: China Storms Africa," *Fast Company,* June 2008.

32.   Richard Behar, "China's New Oil Supplier," *Fast Company*, June 2008.

33.   Gary Fields, "The High School Dropout's Economic Ripple Effect," *Wall Street Journal,* October 21, 2008.

34.   American Youth Policy Forum, "Whatever It Takes: How Twelve Communities Are Reconnecting Out-of-School Youth," www.aypf.org/publications/WhateverItTakes/WIT_nineseconds.pdf.

35.   John Stuart Mill, *On Liberty and Other Essays* (Oxford University Press, 1998), 2-3.

36.   U.S. Census Bureau.

37.   U.S. Department of Education, National Center for Education Statistics. (2010). The Condition of Education 2010 (NCES 2010-028)

38.   See The Overseas Development Institute's report of June 2010 - The Economic Impact of School Violence: A Report for "Plan International" section 2.1

39.   U.S. Department of Education, *Digest of Education Statistics*, 2008. Table 403 available at http://nces.ed.gov/programs/digest/d08/tables/dt08_403.asp.

40.   U.S. Department of Education, *Digest of Education Statistics*, 2005. Table 391 available at http://nces.ed.gov/programs/digest/d05/tables/dt05_391.asp

41.   Organization for Economic Cooperation and Development, Society at a Glance 2009—OECD Social Indicators, May 2009. Available at www.oecd.org/document/24/0,3343,en_2649_34637_2671576_1_1_1_1,00.html.

42.   "The G.I. Bill and the transformation of America," National Forum, Fall 1995 by Wilson, Reginald.

43.   OECD Programme for International Student Assessment, "The High Cost of Low Educational Performance," 2006.

44. Alliance for Excellent Education, FactSheet March 2008, "How Does the United States Stack Up? International Comparisons of Academic Achievement," available at www.all4ed.org/files/IntlComp_FactSheet.pdf

45. Morgan Tanabe, "U.S. Students Fail Citizenship Test," The State Press (Arizona State University), March 4, 2010. ˜www.statepress.com/2010/03/04/u-s-students-fail-citizenship-test/

46. Report available at www.americancivicliteracy.org.

47. "TV-Free America," report by A.C. Nielsen, Co., in 2008; statistics compiled by TV-Free America; 1322 18th Street, NW ; Washington, DC 20036.

48. Martin Luther King, Jr., "Beyond Vietnam—A Time to Break Silence," Delivered 4 April 1967, Riverside Church, New York City.

49. Martin Luther King, Jr., I Have a Dream," delivered at Lincoln Memorial during March on Washington, D.C., August 28, 1963.

50. (Jagadeesh Gokhale has also made thoughtful contributions).

51. What Every American Needs to Know about Government-Entitlement Reform By Andrew G. Biggs AEI Online (September 2010).

52. What Every American Needs to Know about Government-Entitlement Reform By Andrew G. Biggs AEI Online (September 2010).

53. W.E.B. DuBois, "Closed Ranks," July 1918, Crisis (published by NAACP).

54. Patrick Brady, "The Act of Remembering Grows Patriotism," Express-News.

55. P. 223.

56. Adlai Stevenson, speech to the American Legion convention, New York City, August 27, 1952.

57. Mark Thompson, "The Case for National Service: Would National Service Be Better than the Draft?" Time Magazine, August 30, 2007.

58. The current United States Oath of Allegiance: I hereby declare, on oath, that I absolutely and entirely renounce and abjure all allegiance and fidelity to any foreign prince, potentate, state, or sovereignty of whom or which I have heretofore been a subject or citizen; that I will support and defend the Constitution and laws of the United States of America against all enemies, foreign and domestic; that I will bear true faith and allegiance to the same; that I will bear arms on behalf of the United States when required by the law; that I will perform noncombatant service in the Armed Forces of the United States when required by the law; that I will perform work of national importance under civilian direction when required by the law; and that I take this obligation freely without any mental reservation or purpose of evasion; so help me God.

59. See: The Anglican Library - J.C. (John Charles) Ryle, The Duties of Parents.

60. Dr. Gilbert Morris wrote the book for LeadAmerica which was sold exclusively to students. Used copies are available on Amazon.com.

61. National Scientific Council on the Developing Child (2007). The Timing and Quality of Early Experiences Combine to Shape the Brain Architecture: Working Paper No. 5 Retrieved from www.developingchild.harvard.edu .

62. Arthur J. Rolnick and Rob Grunewald, "The Economics of Early Childhood Education as Seen by Two Fed Economists," Community Investments (published by the San Francisco Federal Reserve), Fall 2007.

63. James Heckman and Dimitriy V. Masterov, "The Productivity Argument for Investing in Young Children," National Bureau of Economic Research, NBER Working Paper No. 13016, April 2007.

64. William Damon, "What Schools Should Do to Prepare Students for Democracy," CIRCLE Working Paper 45—Youth Civic Engagement: An Institutional Turn, February 2006, Center for Information & Research on Civic Learning & Engagment.

65. This quote is always attributed to Burke, however, it cannot be found in Burke's writings.

66. Edmund Burke, Thoughts On The Cause Of The Present Discontents (1770)

INDEX

National Association of Manufacturers, 122
national debt
    budget deficit, 98–100
    debt-to-GDP ratio, 100–102
    held by foreign nations, 104–6
    historical view, 100–101
    interest on, 98, 102–3
    Treasury bond spreads and, 103–4
nationalism versus patriotism, 46–47
National Junior Leaders Conference, 74
National Labor Relations Board, 36
national service
    benefits of, 157–58
    foreign examples of, 158–59
    gratitude and sacrifice values, 145–46
    McCain's sacrifice, 148–49, 151–52
    military option for, 156
    model of, 159–62
    patriotism and, 155
    in practice of founding values, 164
    sacrifice recognition, 146–48
    Stockdale's sacrifice, 149–52
National Student Leadership
    Conference, 74
NATO, 40–41
natural resources, 111–13
Nelson, Charles A., 171
neuroscience, 169–72
New York state, 90, 139
New Zealand, 137

O

Obama, Barack, 97, 108, 136
oil exploration and production, 112–13
Organization for Economic Cooperation and Development (OECD), 97, 120–22
Outliers (Gladwell), 125
Over Here (Humes), 120

P

parenting and entitlement attitudes
    adversity to adversity, 69–70, 75–77
    child-rearing and, 165, 166
    global perspective, 79–81
    narcissism and, 63, 66–67, 166
    teachable moments, 77–79
parents
    child-rearing roles of, 169–72
    family role in education, 125
    teaching about founding values, 164–67, 182
    teaching about respect and honor, 172–75
    teaching about sacrifice and gratitude, 167–69
patriotism
    definition of, 155
    nationalism versus, 46–47
    sacrifice and, 148, 149
    teaching, 178–82
Patterson, David, 90
paying it forward, 185–86
Pay it Forward (Hyde), 185
Peace Corps, 160
Pelosi, Nancy, 91
pension plans, 88–90, 136. See also Social Security
Perot, Ross, 151
Perry Pre-School Program, 177
personal debt, 67, 73, 75
personal responsibility
    adversity aversion and, 68, 70
    American Paradigm and, 26–29
    American values of, 2, 6, 8–9, 11
    avoidance of, 72–74
    as educational principle, 124–25
    entitlement and, 61–62, 64, 65, 74, 131–33, 143–44
    gratitude and, 153–54
    of immigrants, 10, 153–54
    implementation of, 131–32
    inspiration or desperation, 132

ABOUT THE AUTHORS

Chris Salamone is a respected attorney, educator, and thought leader. He is one of the nation's foremost experts on next generation leadership. A serial entrepreneur, Mr. Salamone founded, built, and sold three successful businesses over the past thirteen years. He is co-founder and Chairman of the Board of Spartan Capital Investors, a private investment firm where he works with entrepreneurs and executives to help them achieve their business and financial goals. He is a founding member of the Board of Directors and President/Chief Operating Officer of Chasin Music Group and Chasin Records, and serves on the Advisory Board for Penn-Florida Companies, a full service real estate development and management company. Mr. Salamone has previously served on the advisory boards of several non-profits and multi-national organizations, including the International Advisory Board for Bentley College and the Board of Directors of the Florence Fuller Child Development Centers, as special advisor to the Landfall Centre for Finance, Trade & International Affairs, and to the former Chairman of TC Invest, the National Investment Agency of Turks and Caicos.

Mr. Salamone has dedicated much of his adult life to creating and developing educational and leadership development programs for our nation's youth and young adults. These programs have provided opportunities for students to grow and develop themselves personally and academically. A true visionary, Mr. Salamone created "first of their kind" businesses that have impacted the lives of hundreds of thousands of students and young adults across the country and around the world.

Mr. Salamone is the Founder and former CEO of LeadAmerica, and the National Student Leadership Conference, non-partisan educational organizations that sponsor academic-based leadership programs for high-achieving middle and high school students. He is also the Founder and former President of the National Institute for Legal Education and the BarBri Law Prep Program. He is the co-author of The Law School Companion and author of a lecture tape series on success strategies. Mr. Salamone has taught trial advocacy at Loyola Law School in Chicago, served on the teaching faculty for the National Institute of Trial Advocacy at Nova University Law School and has lectured for various organizations at universities across the country including Stanford, Harvard, the University of Texas, Columbia, and Georgetown.

As Chairman of the LeadAmerica Foundation, and through his personal philanthropy, hundreds of thousands of dollars have been donated to education and leadership development. Through the Foundation, Mr. Salamone founded and sponsors GirlsLead, a non-profit and non-partisan leadership development program for outstanding young women from the US and abroad. Internationally, Mr. Salamone sponsors and provides direct financial support for the education of more than 200 Haitian children. Books, teachers, and other needed supplies are provided as a result of Mr. Salamone's support.

Mr. Salamone is trained in the martial arts of Jyu Ryu and Miyama Ryu Combat Jujitsu. He also enjoys golf, cooking and has a passion for studying and singing opera.

Professor Gilbert Morris is a graduate of Oxford Brookes University with a double BA in Law and Political Science. He has studied at Harvard University's Extension School and was an Institute of British and Irish Studies Scholar in Law at Mansfield College, Oxford. He holds a post-graduate diploma from Cadmus College of Law, London and a research degree from the London School of Economics. He was a visiting professor at George Mason University and a member of the Mid-Atlantic Scholars at Princeton University. He is a member of the Convocation at the University of London, a Fellow of Sir William Goodenough College, London, and a Fellow of the Royal Society of Fellows. Morris served as an advisor to the Minister of Foreign Affairs of the Bahamas, and to the Deputy Premier and Minister of Finance of the Turks & Caicos.